THE MECHANICS OF ANIME AND MANGA

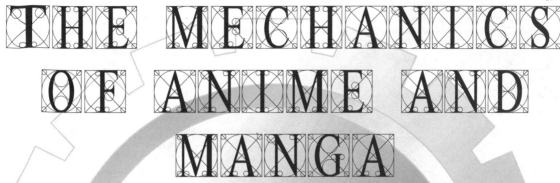

Volume 1: Drawing an Anime or Manga Character from Concept to Color

Studio Imagiks

Wordware Publishing, Inc.

Michelle Lam

Library of Congress Cataloging-in-Publication Data

Drawing an anime-manga character from concept to color / by Studio Imagiks.
    p. cm. -- (The mechanics of anime and manga ; v. 1)
    Includes index.
    ISBN-13: 978-1-59822-019-3 (pbk.)
    ISBN-10: 1-59822-019-5 (pbk.)
    1. Comic books, strips, etc.--Japan--Technique.   2. Cartoon characters--Japan.
    3. Cartooning--Technique. I. Studio Imagiks. II.
    Series.

    NC1764.5.J3D73 2006
    741.5'1--dc22
                                2006013348
                                CIP

ISBN-13: 978-1-59822-019-3
ISBN-10: 1-59822-019-5

10 9 8 7 6 5 4 3 2 1
0606

All inquiries for volume purchases of this book should be addressed to Wordware Publishing, Inc., at the above address. Telephone inquiries may be made by calling:

(972) 423-0090

Preface

Commercial art, as well as fine art, has always reflected the fads and trends of the popular culture of its time. As each trend develops, moves, and fades, the artist or designer must also evolve or be left behind to stagnate. Eventually, those who are afraid of change and controversy will likely be forgotten or, at the very least, forced to leave the cutting edge of art and design.

Over the centuries, many artists have created art that was originally intended for commercial use, only to have it evolve into fine art over time. At times their art would spark social debate and controversy about the state of the overcommercialization of the images, society, and culture around them.

The controversy over commercial vs. fine art has helped to change the face of art over the last two centuries. With the introduction of computers as an art tool, one needs to consider entertainment imagery as a completely separate facet of art and design. This is something that is, once again, sure to change the art scene as we now know it.

In the late 1800s, Toulouse-Lautrec illustrated images of dancers and patrons at the famous Moulin Rouge and other cabarets in Paris. His drawings and paintings became widely sought after as promotional posters for those same cabarets and then as fine art for later generations. His work, as well as Alphonse Mucha's series of promotional posters and prints of the same era, helped define the artistic trends and popular culture for the period. Several generations later they were considered fine art when viewed out of context. In contrast, artists like Norman Rockwell, the preeminent artist of life and the American family of the '30s and '40s, created compelling works of art that could stand alone as fine art. However, they were used as ads, posters, and covers. It was not until later that these images evolved into cultural icons representing the collective emotion and spirit of the America of his time. In our opinion, it is very hard at times to definitively pinpoint where commercial illustration ends and fine art begins. Both are influenced, if not completely determined, by the society, culture, and time period in which they are created. In our globally connected information age, this condition is changing rapidly.

In the years that followed, many artists would find themselves either creating what was to become the pop art of their generation or producing work within the already established trends of their day. In the 1960s and '70s, artists like Roy Lichtenstein and Peter Max emerged. Both worked within the already established trends and popular imagery of their time and then brought their interpretations of those images to new heights. Lichtenstein took the common comic book image to the level of fine art. Max gave visual color and movement to the voices of a whole generation and helped further blur the differences between fad, commercial illustration, and fine art. "Op art," or optical art (named for its illusion of motion), was coined as a description of Max's style. Just as Mucha and Lautrec had done almost a century before, his style moved easily between fine art and commercial illustration. They had broad popular acceptance of the culture, or in Max's case counterculture, of their day.

iii

Meanwhile, Andy Warhol took the images of overcommercialized, American cultural icons found around him and brought them back to their basics of form and color. Using these images, Warhol commented on the American culture's fanatical devotion to trends and fads of the moment and their fickle nature of disposing of them for the next new thing.

This brings us to the question: What is going to be the dominant art movement for the beginning of the new millennium (or at least "the next new thing" right now)? We believe it will be animation in all its present and future forms—art imitating life in 2D, 3D, and beyond. This art form, along with the advancement of computer graphics in general, will lead us to a completely new way of experiencing art.

Currently, the prevalent form of 2D animation is anime (or is at least influenced by the anime style). We believe it will remain the dominant style for some time to come due to the effect it has had on at least one worldwide generation already. It has shown no signs of slowing down.

With the movement toward a world economy and the advent of the Internet, the standard preconceived notion of "what is art" is being challenged on a global scale. Artists are now influenced by thoughts, ideas, and images on a planetary basis more than ever in the history of mankind.

By the same token, the pop culture movement has become a worldwide phenomenon, and is affected by more than any one country, culture, or geographical region. As such, we as artists can now explore, affect, and be affected by other cultures' ideas of what is "popular." This allows "art" to be viewed at a more individual level instead of the societal level of an artist's specific culture. In our opinion, anime is a prime example of this and we believe it is becoming one of the first pop art forms accepted on a global scale. It is because of this movement that we feel that images with an anime flair, animated or otherwise, should be embraced as "the next big thing" to come along. We, as an advertising design studio competing for a share of the market, are experimenting with the use of anime along with other pop art styles, past and present. We are exploring the many applications in which they can be adapted for today's and tomorrow's mainstream commercial needs.

For professional and amateur artists alike, the adaptation of anime and manga (the print form of anime) into commercially and/or socially relevant and acceptable imagery can be far simpler than it may seem. Many aspects of the style have already been adapted or "commercialized" for the American market through television series like *Xao Lin Showdown* or *Teen Titans*. Every month there are dozens of conventions held annually in small towns and big cities throughout the country that also spread anime as an accepted art form. Although shows and events like these embody only a small part of the anime style, they have effectively opened the door for today's commercial and pop artist to explore its uses within an already established consumer base.

Anime is no longer just the stereotypical "big eyes, small mouths." With an audience ever expanding in age and scope, in conjunction with the art form itself evolving into new "alternative styles," the possibilities are endless. So, unfortunately, are the complications. You may have questions like "What defines anime?" or "How do I adopt an anime or manga style to my or my client's needs?" These are just some of the questions we hope to address with our "The Mechanics of Anime and Manga" series.

To begin, you can simply explore and identify a character style that you believe will work for your needs. (Avoid the exact duplication of any specific character.) This can be done by anyone, and can be good practice while developing your own individual style. Adapting one's own drawing style to that of anime can necessitate a shift in one's perception of what is and is not acceptable as good design.

Anime, like previous pop art styles, is a highly graphic reinterpretation or "stylization" of life, its figures, creatures, environments, etc. The way in which the Japanese have adapted their particular look has given anime a unique and interesting stylistic feel. It has a fresh, strong, graphic, and contemporary look that adapts well across the full spectrum of popular art and advertising design.

Disney cartoons of the 1920s and '30s influenced early Japanese animators like Osama Tezuka, who adapted the large Disney-style eyes into characters for the animated series *Astroboy* and *Metropolis*. They set the precedent for the large, expressive, anime eyes we see today. Later, animators would be influenced and even trained by the simplicity of Hanna-Barbera character designs that contrasted with the quality of their complex movements.

Other widely distributed animes include Hayao Miyazaki and Studio Ghibli's *Howl's Moving Castle*, *Spirited Away*, and *Princess Mononoke*. All of these films were released in the American market under Disney's distribution. Another anime, *Vampire Hunter D: Bloodlust*, was produced and distributed in the United States.

Anime phenomena like *Pokemon* and *Dragonball Z* have further popularized the look. These titles, coupled with lesser-known but equally wonderful movies like *Millennium Actress*, have given birth to a whole new wave of anime fans and created a rich and varied fan base. This setup is perfect for anyone wanting to produce images with this generation's pop culture and purchasing power in mind.

Introduction

The imagery of popular culture is often the breeding ground for both commercial and fine art. Cultural fads and trends often have a direct effect on art and design. Over time they can become the iconic representations of that culture. Later they could stand on their own as great works of art. At the same time in the Internet age, commercial fads and trends are becoming a global effect. Fortunes are made or lost by the prediction of what will be "hot" five minutes in the future.

With the simple turn of a magazine page or the flip of a TV channel, the public's interests can change. Popular tastes and perceptions can also come full circle only to reappear later as retro or "old school." As artists we should be open to these changes with a willingness to experience and explore the popular movements ebbing and flowing around us.

We find anime to be the dominant example of the present form of this movement and expect it to stay that way for some time to come. In our "The Mechanics of Anime and Manga" series, we would like to explore the fundamental hallmarks of this art form and several of the possible applications of its style for today's professional, amateur, and hobby artist.

For the purposes of these books, we suggest that you have some prior knowledge of the basics of drawing and applications of color. This includes, but is not limited to, computer-based paint and drawing programs like Adobe Photoshop or Corel Painter. We will also touch on the traditional methods of paper, pencil, ink, and marker.

While we will give a brief overview of the use of some of the most popular computer imaging programs, this is for informational purposes only. We do not want to suggest that any one program or the computer itself should ever become a replacement for actual hands-on experience with your drawing and/or coloring mediums of choice.

In our design studio, the computer is the one tool we use most and find indispensable in today's fast-paced digital age. With that said, all our concepts still originate from a series of traditionally hand-drawn sketches. That is something that we will never change. We feel that there is not enough said for a firm foundation in traditional methods and the need for their use in all forms of art.

We would also like to say that the methods and techniques presented in this book series are the best way we have found for us to adapt the anime and manga styles for our professional and personal use. We are not implying this is the only or best way. These are just the ways we found that have worked the best for us after years of trial and error. As such, we believe this information may help anyone interested in adapting the anime and manga styles for their own uses.

Keep in mind that while this book covers several types of anime and manga styles, it is not meant to cover all styles in use today. Not all anime is big eyes and small mouths, just as not all American animation is Disney or Hanna-Barbera. Some anime, such as *Sin* and *Akira*, is actually very close to American animation. To cover all styles of anime would take far more than this series of books could possibly cover and would require the far more extensive expertise of the Japanese creators themselves.

Our purpose for this series of books is to explore the many uses of this art style, such as its use in mainstream advertising as well as its contributions to today's pop culture. These books will also be of great interest to those who want nothing more than the simple pleasure of exploring and drawing in this popular style.

We hope you enjoy using the books as much as we enjoyed creating them. We also hope you come away better informed—or at least entertained—for having read them.

WELCOME

Welcome to volume one of "The Mechanics of Anime and Manga" series: *Drawing an Anime or Manga Character from Concept to Color*. My name is KiKi and this is Menmou. We'll be your guides through this series! We hope you enjoy this book and have fun!

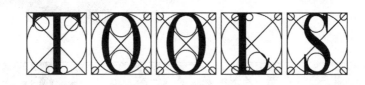

- Blue Line Pencil
- Drafting Pencils
- Technical Pens, Pigment Pens, and Brushes
- Markers and Colored Pencils
- T-Squares, Triangles, and French Curves
- Computers

Tools

The tools you use to draw with are as important as the techniques that are used. While most of the tools are general to almost all forms and styles of art, some are more stylized in their use.

Many specialized tools normally found in the graphic design field can be used for all forms of drawing including the anime style. Tools like blue line and drafting pencils find multiple purposes in such things as laying the foundation of an image and preparing your piece for inking.

Blue Line Pencil

A blue line pencil is a tool used for the preliminary conceptualization of your drawings. A handy little tool, the blue line pencil (also known as non-repro blue) gives a light blue line. In the days before computers, blue line pencils allowed you to do preliminary drawings that could later be inked over. When photocopied, the blue would drop out, leaving a clean inked image. Blue pencil is generally used for lines of action and roughs. This is further discussed in Chapter 5, "Posing and Movement." You could either pencil or ink over the blue. However, in the anime style, blue lines can also be used as borders for shadows, which can be filled and covered.

Blue line pencil is the tool we use for under drawing, though not exclusively. As such, a well-sharpened blue pencil (or a number 2H graphite) is a must. If you have a mechanical pencil, be sure to have the proper size and type of lead. The exception to this would be for print-oriented or conceptual pieces, which can be done with several inking styles over a light 2H pencil or a light computer printout.

Be careful! Some stores or retailers will try to pass off a blue pencil for the true blue line/col-erase pencils. To be on the safe side, test a pencil or ask to see a sample of what its line looks like. If the pencil leaves behind a light line, even with heavy pressure, it is a true blue line pencil. If the line it leaves behind is dark and thick, thank the dealer and move on.

(A blue line pencil is shown on the next page with the drafting pencils.)

Drafting Pencils

Drafting pencils are more useful in the conceptual stages than the actual animation stages. However, they are essential for character designs, especially those in grayscale.

Drafting pencils come in sets of varying hardness. Though you can buy individual pencils as replacements for those you go through quicker, a good set of drafting pencils, with a range of at least six degrees of hardness, will last an artist a fairly good while.

One method we have found for creating texture in a computer color rendering is to create a grayscale value study in pencil. You then scan it into a computer and apply color to it in varying degrees of transparency using one of the popular raster manipulation programs. (Refer to Chapter 2, "Programs.") This gives you a textural effect under your color, which can add drama to your final piece.

Pencils are graded by degrees of hardness. 2H-6H are the hard, light pencils. 6H is the hardest and lightest of the H pencils. F is the hardest and lightest of drafting pencils. 2B-6B are the softer and darker pencils with 2B being the darkest. A 2HB is your standard, general-use number 2 pencil.

The various pencil grades can be used to create a layering effect of dark and light grays for value studies, shadowing, texturing, and line work. They are also essential for people with different drawing styles. For example, a person with a heavy hand might choose to draw with a harder leaded pencil 4H-6H, and a person with a light hand might choose to use a softer leaded pencil 2B-4B. This can done so that the pencil will compensate and lines will still end up crisp and clean on the paper. This minimizes cleanup and saves the artist precious time during the inking phase.

Like many of the tools in this chapter, drafting pencils can be found at many craft or hobby stores as well as stores specifically catering to art professionals. Unlike other specialized drawing tools, drafting pencils can sometimes be found in the arts and hobbies section of many general superstores.

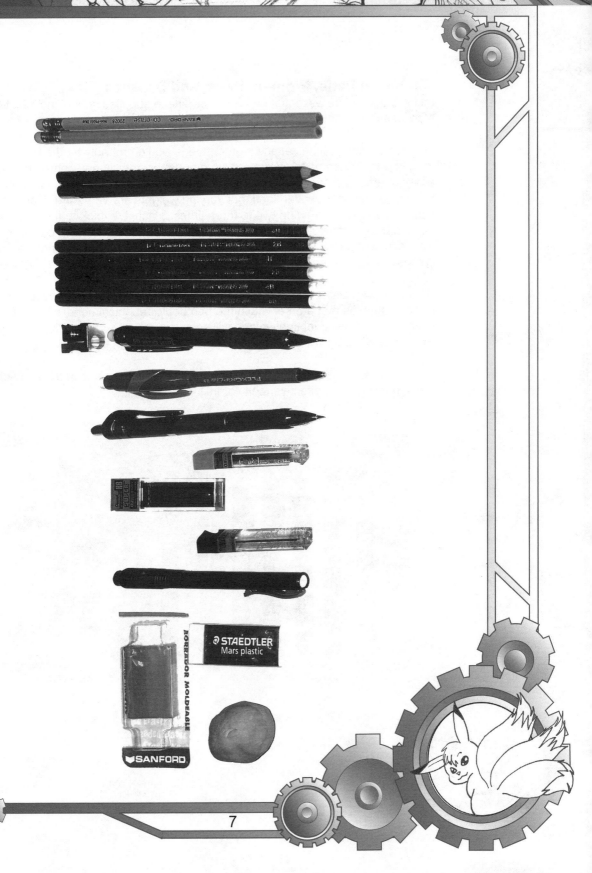

Technical Pens, Pigment Pens, and Brushes

Inking supplies are essential for any artist. These supplies should include: technical pens, pigment pens, brushes, and ink.

For the beginner, technical and pigment pens would probably be the best choice to start with. These pens offer a certain amount of stability and control for the amateur artist that brush inks cannot. However, some people find that pens have so much control over lines that varying weights are very hard to achieve. One can go over a drawing two to three times to achieve thick-to-thin lines. Also, ink and brush techniques make filling large areas with black much easier than with technical pens. Technical pens usually have to surrender to markers when it comes to large spaces.

Technical pens differ from pigment pens in the types of inks that they lay on paper and the nibs that are set within the pen body. Technical pens, while offering a stable and consistent line weight, will snap and fray over time. Pigment pens, while they will still fray, will gradually soften into almost a brush tip.

Technical pens and pigment pens, as with brushes, also come in a variety of sizes, making them effective tools for inking.

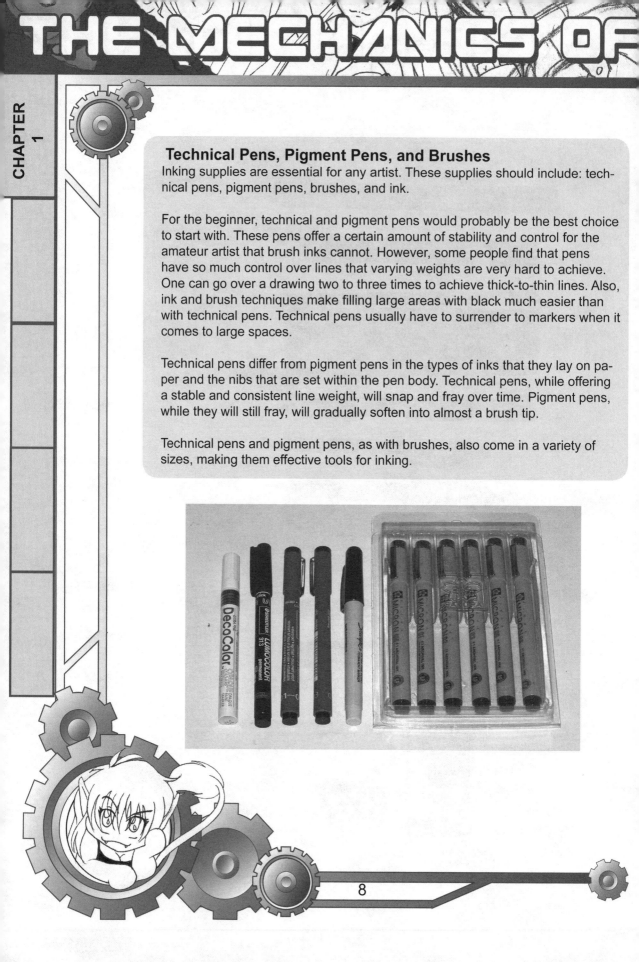

Markers and Colored Pencils

Traditionally, color comps (or roughs taken from a sketch up through the finishing process) were done with either markers (designer markers; that is, ones that are alcohol based rather than water based) or professional-grade colored pencils. However, with the advent of computers and computer painting programs with layering systems, you can scan your images directly to the computer.

Markers that are considered industry standard are solvent based (generally using either alcohol or benzene as a carrier). The upsides to markers are that they can be refilled a limited number of times, require no electricity, are blendable, come in a wide variety of colors, and are much cheaper than a computer system and painting software. The downsides to markers are that they can streak, are permanent, and cost more than colored pencils or standard markers. Additionally, it is harder to cover up mistakes and, while they are reputed to be refillable, the nibs can wear out with vigorous use.

The main benefit of colored pencils is that they are cheaper than markers. They are capable of creating softer blends while keeping the portability of a non-digital medium. Colored pencils have a broad color spectrum that is at least as widespread as professional markers. They can be blended with their blenders as well as marker blenders, or you can use isopropyl alcohol and a cotton swab to blend. Colored pencils, however, are problematic when rendering lighting effects and can be very difficult to master.

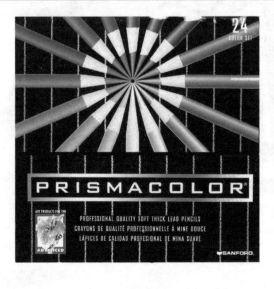

T-Squares, Triangles, and French Curves

T-squares, triangles, and French curves are support material used for drawing clean straight or curved lines. Although these tools are primarily used for architectural designs, we will be using them for perspective and organic shapes. T-squares give you a straight and level edge to draw perfectly straight lines when used in conjunction with a support structure such as a drawing board or drawing table that has a smooth, clean, straight edge. A T-square is also used as a support edge for the triangle. Triangles are used for specific angles. There is a 30-60-90 degree triangle and a 45 degree triangle (all three corners are 45 degrees). When used with a T-square, this gives you the ability to draw a clean, straight line at 30, 45, 60, and 90 degrees. French curves are used to make organic shapes as opposed to straight lines and angles. You can usually find French curves in plastic and in sets of three to five. These are used to make clean lines in curves or in curved areas.

While these tools are not as widely used in character creation, they will be extensively used in our second book on environmental creation.

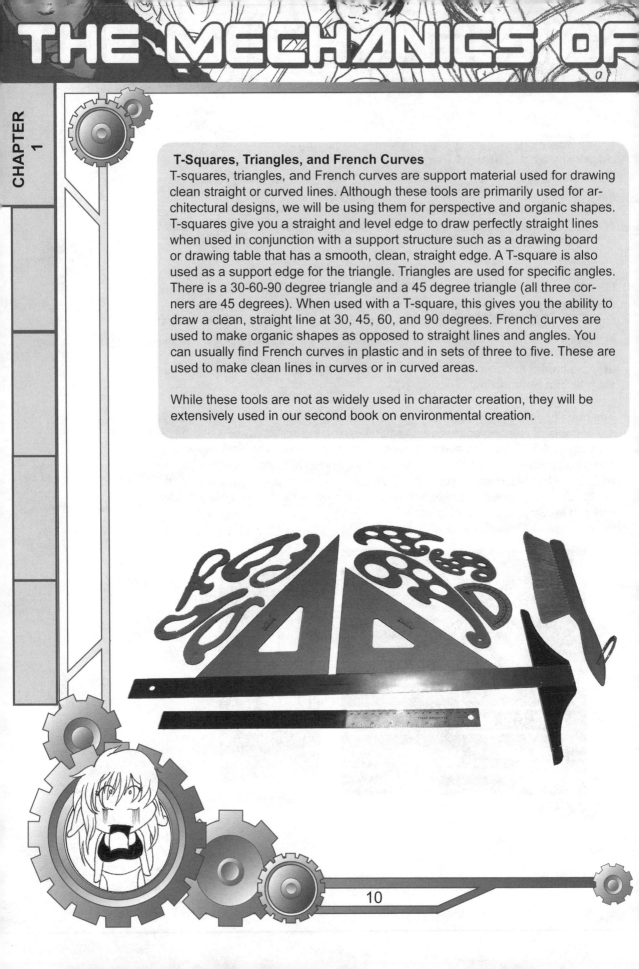

Computers

A computer system incorporating a scanner, a painting program, and an input device (either a mouse or a stylus/tablet) is probably the most versatile of all methods. A computer makes changing details far easier and faster than with traditional media. A computer can also save several different versions of an image for future reference or concept development. The downside of a computer system is the price. The cheapest of computer systems can still cost hundreds of dollars, not including software; they directly (tower/desktop) or indirectly (laptops) require electricity; and while laptops can afford some level of portability, they will eventually need recharging and are more expensive up front.

All of these systems require time to research and practice, and artists should take the time to choose the one best for them.

PROGRAMS

2

- Raster vs. Vector
- Adobe Photoshop
- Adobe Illustrator

Programs

In this chapter we discuss the pros and cons of the two different types of programs in the application of line and color. We also have a short discussion on raster vs. vector. Adobe Photoshop and Corel Painter are raster based, while Adobe Illustrator and Corel Draw are vector-based programs. We are not suggesting that Adobe is the only program manufacturer you should consider (though they are the most predominant standards in the industry); there are many other versatile and capable programs available on the market. First and foremost would be Corel Painter and Corel Draw, but for the purposes of this book, we will be focusing on Adobe Photoshop and Illustrator.

VECTOR Rastor

VEC1 Rast

VER2

Raster vs. Vector

Photo editing and painting programs work on a raster system. Loosely defined, a raster system assigns a square of color (defined as a pixel) to a given area. The number of pixels per inch is abbreviated as PPI (pixels per inch) or, in printing terminology, DPI (dots per inch). The higher this number is, the clearer the image will appear. The densities of pixels, whether from far away or zoomed in, will create a seamless and integrated image.

72 dpi

300 dpi

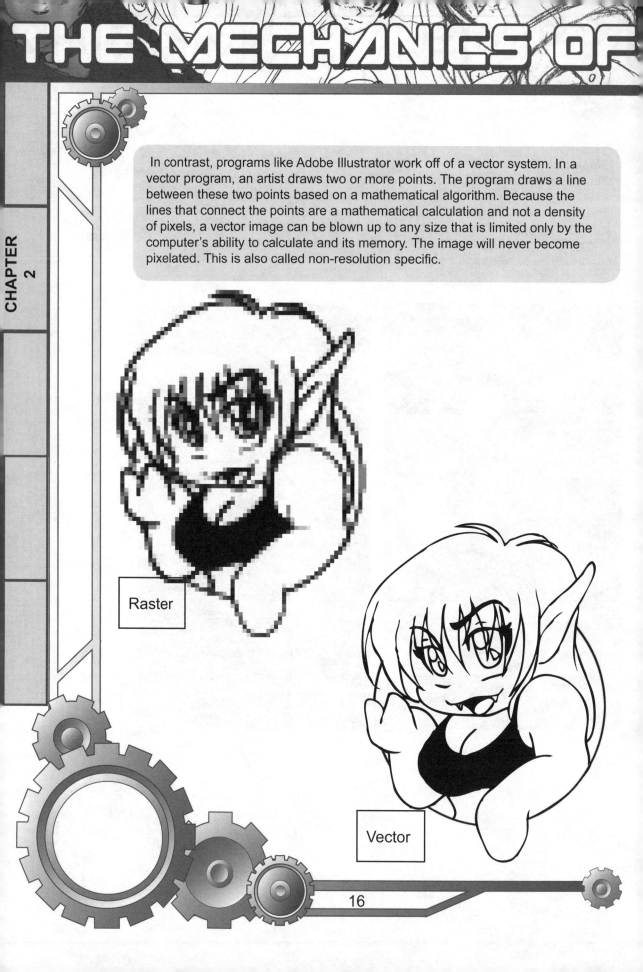

In contrast, programs like Adobe Illustrator work off of a vector system. In a vector program, an artist draws two or more points. The program draws a line between these two points based on a mathematical algorithm. Because the lines that connect the points are a mathematical calculation and not a density of pixels, a vector image can be blown up to any size that is limited only by the computer's ability to calculate and its memory. The image will never become pixelated. This is also called non-resolution specific.

Raster

Vector

Adobe Photoshop

Adobe Photoshop is Adobe's premier image manipulation and computer coloring system. It is a program whose roots are based in the photography industry. Adobe Photoshop evolved from photo editing into a sophisticated image editing and paint program featuring many innovative and time-saving techniques.

One of these features is Photoshop's layering system. This system permits you to assign a piece of a composition or drawing to a layer. This can be likened to tracing paper. After drawing an image, one can overlay another piece of paper over the original and draw another element while still able to see the underlying piece of paper. Photoshop's layer system works in very much the same way, with the added ability to adjust the opacity levels of the layers to modify their visibility.

With layers you can lay an element or image over another. By manipulating opacity you can allow one layer a greater or lesser visibility to the layers above and below it. This is much in the same way a traditional animator layers cels to make a piece of an image. Pieces on a layer that cannot be seen through are opaque. Sections of the layer that can be partially seen through and have colored elements are translucent.

Like all computer programs, Photoshop allows the user to save multiple versions of a piece, just in case the artist wishes to revert back to an older version. This comes in handy if, for example, a client liked a previous incarnation of an image better than a more recent one.

 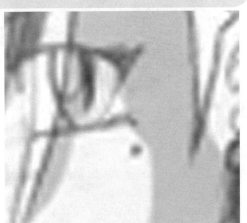

Photoshop's functions are based on a raster system, which assigns a square of color or pixel to a specific place on a canvas. Groups of pixels give the illusion of a solid piece when zoomed out, similar to a mosaic. This system allows many more variations in color and gradation. However, this is detrimental when one tries to enlarge a picture beyond 100%.

As an example of a resolution-specific (or raster-based) effect, place two 1x1" circles side by side. One of these has 72 dots equally sized and equally spaced. The other has 300 dots, also equally sized and equally spaced. The one with more dots would have to have the dots (or pixels) closer together, which creates a denser field of color, especially when compared to the one with fewer dots. This also allows for the greater percentages of enlargement that can be attained before the field breaks up (pixelates) and creates a fuzzy or out of focus effect. 300 DPI can be enlarged to 200% with minimal loss of apparent clarity.

If you enlarge the same image over 200%, it pixelates in direct proportion to the percentage of increase. In other words, an 8x8" square of red at 300 DPI could be made into a 16x16" square and still appear as dense and saturated as it did before the enlargement. At 72 DPI, you can only enlarge an image by about 50% to 75% before the quality of the image is affected.

It is generally accepted that the greater amount of space there is between pixels in an original image, the faster degradation will set in at any amount of enlargement. In essence, the smaller the DPI or PPI, the smaller the percentage of enlargement that can be made before the image begins to break up. 72 DPI/PPI is used as the minimum screen and image resolution. 300 DPI is the minimum for quality print resolution.

Photoshop features things like preserving transparency. This feature is also handy when producing effects for your character, as different transparency levels can give a dramatic feeling to a piece. Transparency is also commonly used to produce a depth of field effect.

Also featured in Photoshop are lighting effects, texturing effects, and layer effects that are more thoroughly described in your user's manual.

Adobe Illustrator

Adobe Illustrator is the vector counterpart to Adobe Photoshop.

Illustrator's vector capabilities make it a very useful program when rendering in the anime style. By overlaying blocks of color one can achieve the color-on-color look of cel shading on a piece that is infinitely reproducible and infinitely resizable. Because lines in Illustrator are vector and are recalculated each time an image is resized, an Illustrator image will never pixelate.

In CS2 (the latest incarnation of Adobe Illustrator), several levels of auto vectorization are featured. This makes vectorizing anime cel-art and inked drawings easier than ever.

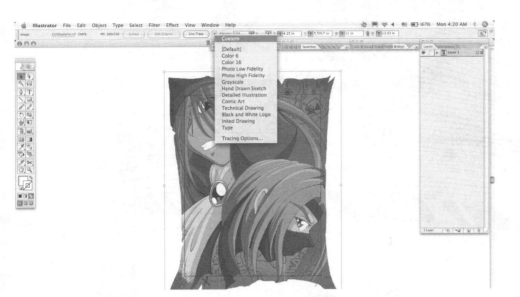

The versatility of Illustrator doesn't stop there. With set after set of universal color charts and Pantone swatches, the compatibility from computers to printers is even easier. Colors are truer to life and just as vibrant as onscreen views. Colors will also print more truly with the use of those Pantone swatches. Illustrator is a tool used mainly for pieces that are going to need to be enlarged, making it perfect for large flyers, posters, banners, or other promotional projects.

CONCEPT

3

- Anime Archetypes
  - Schoolboys and Schoolgirls
  - Modern Characters for High School Drama
  - Old Characters
  - Cyber or Futuristic Characters
  - Magic Users, Fighters, and Warriors
  - Cat Girls and Dog Boys
  - Monsters
  - Cute and Fluffy Sidekicks

Conceptualization

The first step of any characterization is conceptualization. For the sake of these examples, the conceptualization of a character is defined as the thought process that comes before characterization.

The simplest way to conceptualize is to begin with a string of questions. You should ask yourself questions like:
- How old is this character?
- Is it male or female?
- Is it even human?

Continue your conceptualization with a series of more specific questions. Ask such things as:
- Is the character an antagonist, protagonist, or neutral?
- Is this character an anti-hero or a hero?
- Is he or she the bad boy/girl or the boy/girl next door?
- What are the motivations for the character's actions?
- How would the character respond in certain situations?

For the second stage of conceptualization, take those answers and factor them into the character and consider:
- What will this character need to fulfill its requirements and missions?
- What kind of weapons, armor, or other equipment will he/she need?
- Does he or she have something that gives an edge in fulfilling the mission or does he or she have some handicap to work around?
- What is special about the character that sets it apart from others?
- Does he or she have a birthmark, glasses, cool hair, etc.?

Keep in mind the context of your character. Things like survival and battle would motivate a warrior girl. She needs clothing appropriate to the time period, armor to protect vital areas, and a weapon. In our example, she is in a feudal time period but in a fantasy world. Her armor has been customized and she is not wearing full plate armor because it would hinder movement. Also, her weapon is a light sword to aid in the speed of her attacks.

If one were to ignore the motivation and dress her like a schoolgirl, the odds of somebody immediately pegging her for a warrior are very low. Now that does not mean this cannot be done for comedic or suspenseful effects, but be sure that you take in the side effects of that. Being unarmed, for example, your warrior girl will need to find weapons and armor and such, so you must plan ahead.

Also, realize that the gender of the character (or lack thereof) can affect the character's needs. Females will respond to and require different items and wardrobes for a given situation. Males would have different requirements. Also, characters driven more by animal instinct than a human drive would need completely different things than a human. They might not even require clothes.

For characters completely commercial in nature, the most basic questions will probably suffice, but for more complex characters, you should probably sit down with the client and discuss exactly what motivations and attributes they want to see in the character.

Here's an exercise to help with this. Take a blank sheet of notebook paper. Down one side write a question about the character and answer it. Next to the answer, list the pros and cons of the outcome. Once you start answering the basics (who, what, where, when, why, how or how come), other things will come to light that you may not have considered. Below is an example diagram regarding what we thought about when Kiki was created.

Question	Answer	Pros	Cons
What is the gender of your character?	Female	She has cute dresses and outfits and cuddles with Menmou.	Some might view her or her attitude as frivolous.
How old is your character?	214 years old	Mature enough to handle her responsibilities, while maintaining a lighthearted attitude.	She is considered "old" by human standards but a teenager by her race.
Is the character human? If it is not human, what is it?	She is not human but her race is unspecified.	Kiki is interesting to view and draw with her cute tail, adorable wings, and expressive ears.	She is a little more difficult and time-consuming to draw because of extra body parts. Also, viewers may have a hard time identifying with a nonhuman.
What sort of personality does your character have?	Although usually sweet and happy, you don't want to irritate her!	Her cheerful attitude is refreshing.	Viewers might finde her comments annoying.
Does your character have motivations for what it does?	She wants to help readers understand what the authors are trying to convey.	She is the vessel through which the authors interject silly, snide, and sarcastic comments.	Some might think she is extraneous or inane.
What kinds of clothes does your character need or like?	She likes to wear midriff baring tops and long slitted skirts that match her headband.	Her outfit is cute and fun to draw.	She has to be careful of how she flies or she could flash the people below her.
Can or does your character use a weapon and what is it?	Kiki has a staff, but will usually have a pen or pencil in hand for the book.	Pen and pencils help illustrate a point. She, in fact, can use the staff in a fight and it also helps her cast spells.	A staff might be too stereotypical of magic users.

Anime Archetypes

Archetypes are the most common and usually stereotypical characters in anime. They are the staple of the genre and are usually set apart by very distinct characteristics. In conceptualization it is important to know your characters' goals and which archetype most closely resembles them. Later, they may deviate from the archetype, but it is easier to show an evolution in character when you begin with a template character.

Schoolgirls and Schoolboys

Many anime stories feature teens and young adults in school, and as such, the schoolgirl or boy is a very prominent anime figure. A character in a school uniform already indicates he or she is a young person. There are a few instances where, for example, a centuries-old character will pose as a young person attending school for whatever reason, but that is not too common.

Remember that the type of uniform you put your character in can say as much as if not more than not putting him or her in a uniform at all. Certain uniforms can tell the age of a character (if he or she is in junior high or high school), their status in life (if they are in a rich or poor school), or even the time of year (many uniforms have a summer and a winter version). Do a little research on Japanese schools if you are not completely sure.

A school uniform makes a powerful statement. It can mean, "On top of saving the world every night, I have to take final exams too?!" which would add a lot of stress in a character's life that you as the creator will have to take into account. The character will have to study, attend classes, and do homework assignments just like his or her classmates, or at least enough to keep up appearances if he or she has an alter ego that needs to remain hidden and anonymous. If your character has to travel throughout the world for an adventure, how will he or she make it back in time to turn in a take-home chemistry quiz? These are some things you will have to remember and work with.

Since the character is still in school, the uniform can be interpreted to mean the character is still developing emotionally and so may be sweetly naïve or disturbingly immature. For instance, if you decide your character's romantic interest is the coolest and most sought-after girl in school, then your character may be an absolute klutz or be so shy he can only stammer incoherently around her. Perhaps your character is unable to express his feelings and so comes off as a jerk but only toward his love interest.

Surely you remember your high school years, when you were surrounded in all sorts of drama, either self-inflicted or thrust upon you by friends. Angst is a big part of being a teenager. It can stem from insecurities about one's abilities or from some sort of trauma that has shaped the character's life. Angst is especially prominent in girls' anime and manga, and is usually the center of the story. The act of overcoming this flaw or trauma (or not, in the case of tragedies) is what the character strives for throughout the story.

School uniforms are fun to put characters in and can be a wonderful form of continuity for your manga or anime. However, remember that no one likes to have to wear the same thing over and over again, so occasionally drawing your character in a trendy outfit is never a bad thing!

These girls are usually the shy goody-goody type. They will blush easily and fairly often.

Traditional Schoolgirl

35

Bold and brazen in the face of authority, this girl does as she pleases.

Rebel Schoolgirl

CHAPTER
3

Dependable and honest, traditional schoolboys work hard at their studies but will still help the little old lady across the street with her groceries.

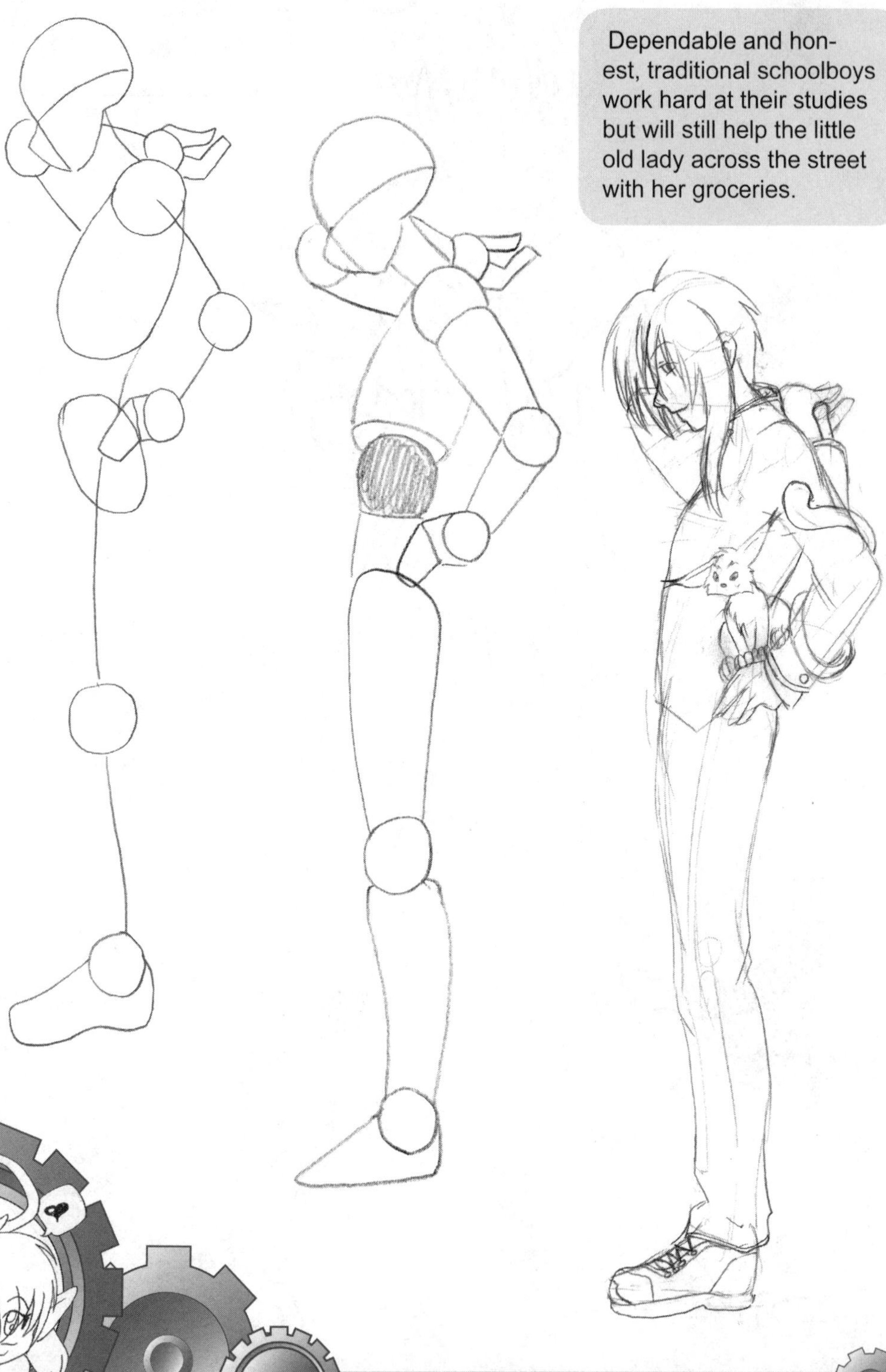

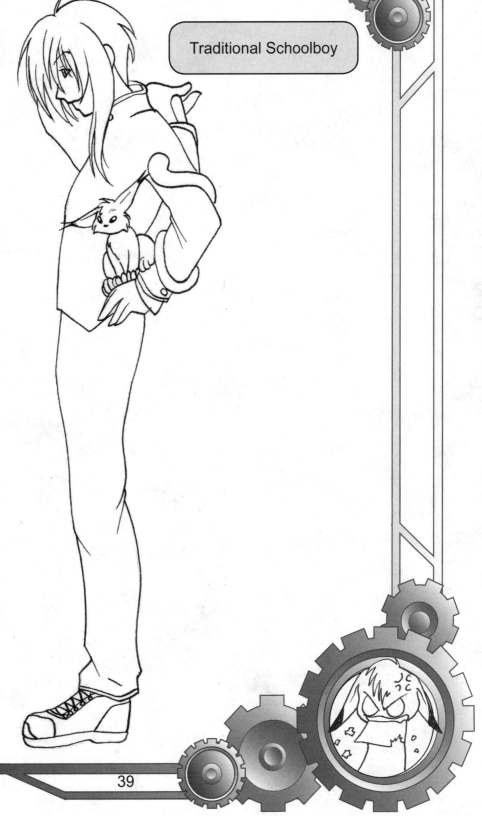

Traditional Schoolboy

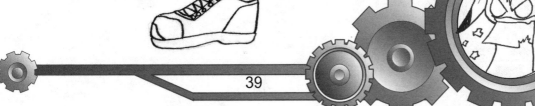

CHAPTER 3

Rules? Hah. This troublemaker thrives on breaking them.

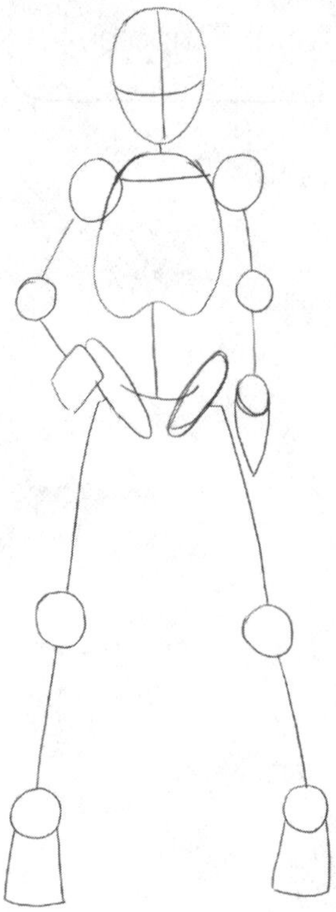

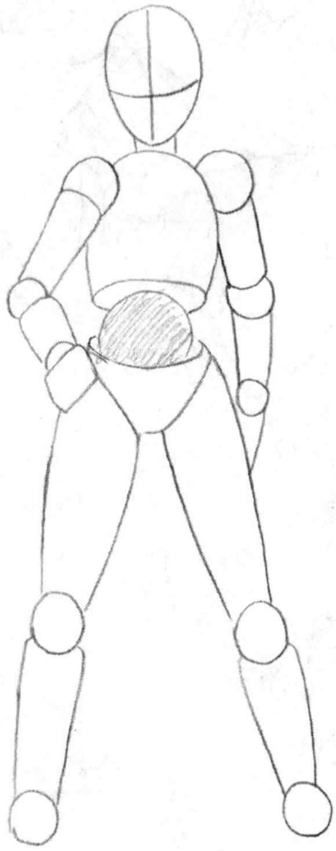

Rebel Schoolboy

CHAPTER
3

Schoolboys and Schoolgirls

Modern Characters for High School Dramas

Your story would probably not be very interesting if you only had just your one main character. You also need to take into consideration others around your character. Who might interact with your character? Who else exists in the world you are creating? The following are just a few specialized genres you would encounter in a high school.

What makes a setting both believable and interesting is a diverse range of people, groups, activities, and so on. Even if your school-age character only hangs out with a specific clique or group, what are his or her interactions with others like? Does he or she treat authority figures with respect?

In most cases with anime and manga, a main character and several supporting characters are forced into a situation in which their skills and traits are all necessary for survival. Therefore, members of different cliques are forced to get along, and somewhere along the way they may even become friends.

Regardless of their relationships with the main character (or maybe one of these archetypes is the main character), these archetypes are far from your ordinary boys and girls on campus. They make up the strange and wondrous inner circles of modern-day high school adventure and mayhem, a deviation from the norm, and a truly three-dimensional cast.

CHAPTER 3

Think of the loudmouthed troublemaker in class. He can be very abrasive and down-right rude at times, but underneath it all he has a heart of gold. Usually he will be pierced and have baggy pants, unruly hair, or some other "bad boy" trait.

Punk

This genre of character refers to the quiet kid who always dresses in black. He is cold and quiet, and seems to try to detach or isolate himself from social situations. He has the best of intentions, but rubs people the wrong way by being too quiet or "creepy."

Goth

He is quiet and has a very shy air. He keeps to himself, but when a subject comes up where his intellect is useful, he shines. He is not afraid to contribute where his talents are concerned.

Geek

Loligoths are typically girls, happy and outspoken but a little off in all respects. She is cute but creepy, happy but sarcastic. The loligoth is a study of opposites.

Loligoth

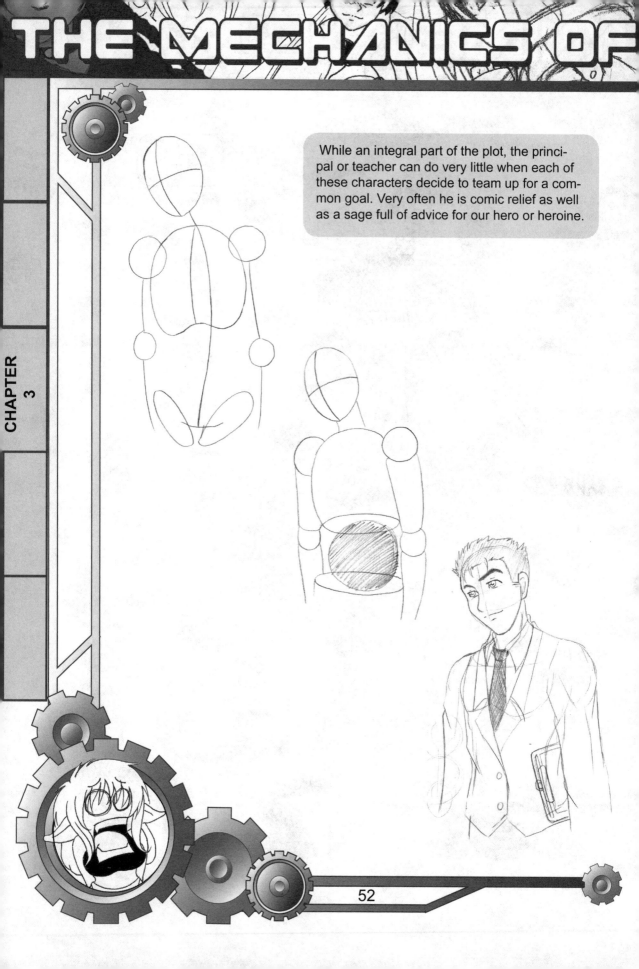

While an integral part of the plot, the principal or teacher can do very little when each of these characters decide to team up for a common goal. Very often he is comic relief as well as a sage full of advice for our hero or heroine.

Principal

53

Modern Characters for High School Drama

Old Characters

With age comes wisdom. At least we hope so! The younger generation looks to its predecessors for example and guidance… sometimes. Old men and women can help guide younger characters with their knowledge, or they can be senile comedic characters. Depending on your character, he or she can receive advice from an older character or can be that older character giving advice.

Whether it is a grandparent, parent, martial arts instructor, professor, or just someone to look up to, a wise mentor can help your character reach understanding. Usually this sort of character will be dignified and command a certain amount of respect from everyone.

Then of course there are the comical elderly. There are the delusional people, such as the old traditional grandmother hell-bent on marrying off her granddaughter to an eligible bachelor or trying to get herself a new husband. There are also the perverted ones that can include the disgusting old man trying to peep at young women or the old crone pinching the buttocks of embarrassed young men. There are many variations of the humorous old man or woman, but the perverted old man and wise, dryly sarcastic crone seem to be the most prevalent.

Senility is a serious issue. It can cause heartache in a character, such as when a grandparent confuses him or her with a deceased parent, for example. On the other end of the spectrum, it can also be used for comedy, such as an old man forgetting his own identity and deciding he wants to be an American cowboy. If you focus on one extreme, it might be best to omit the other since vacillating between the two could confuse a viewer.

Though comical characters are not uncommon, be aware that in Asian cultures, the elderly are given the highest respect.

CHAPTER 3

Ladies, don't let this old gramps behind you! Be wary of his cat-that-ate-the-canary smile.

Lecherous Old Man

The sage's gently benign smile assures you that he indeed has the answers you seek.

Sage Old Man

He's watched you fall and has helped you back on your feet countless times. He is the familiar face that's supported you through your trials.

Mentor Old Man

Don't let her know you're single! It seems she cannot rest until the entire country has been coupled off!

Lecherous Old Woman

Her reputation precedes her. She may not always give you the answer, but she'll at least point you down the path you need.

Sage Old Woman

She is always ready to listen, usually with a pot of hot tea and cookies as you pour out your problems.

Mentor Old Woman

Old Characters

Cyber or Futuristic Characters

Cyborgs, androids, and robots fall into this category. All of the aforementioned have synthetic qualities. Whether biosynthetic or auto mechanical, there is something manmade about these characters.

Cyborgs are humans who have been augmented by technology—sometimes by traumatic events, sometimes by conscious choice. These are organic mechanical hybrids. These characters often have to wrestle with decisions when human nature and cold mechanical logic conflict.

Androids are fully synthetic but have an outward human appearance. A well-made android will be able to blend seamlessly into a crowd.

Robots, however, do not have to look human. They can have humanoid shapes, but cannot blend into a crowd of humans the way androids do. Robots are built to provide a specific function or to perform a specific task.

THE MECHANICS OF

These characters tend to augment themselves with functionality in the forefront of their mind.

Male Cyborg

They blend form and function. In anime, their modifications do not interfere with their femininity or grace.

Female Cyborg

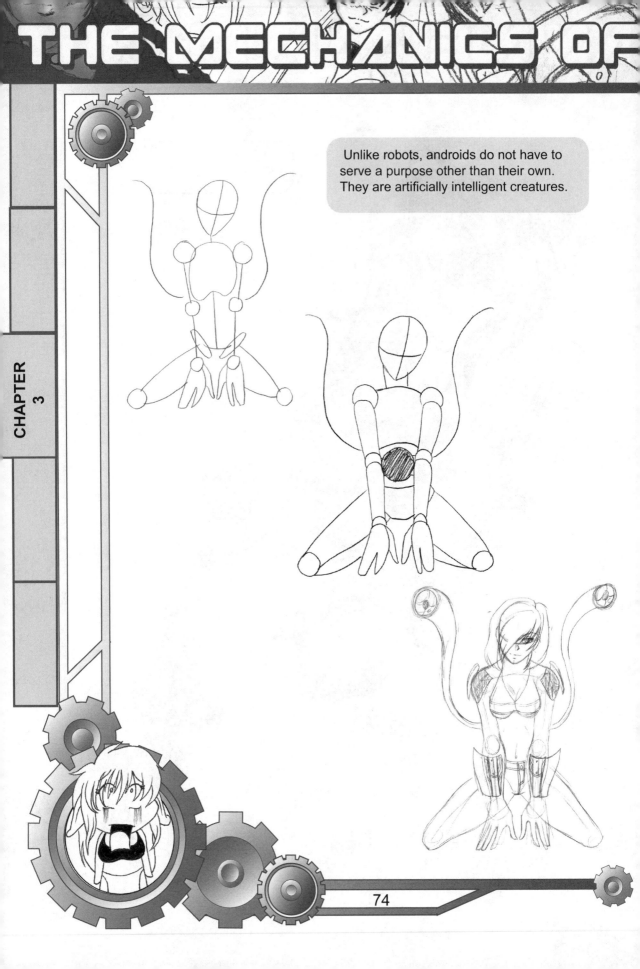

Unlike robots, androids do not have to serve a purpose other than their own. They are artificially intelligent creatures.

CHAPTER 3

Android

Functionality is the primary purpose of a robot. It was made for a reason and will fulfill its purpose until outside influences halt its actions.

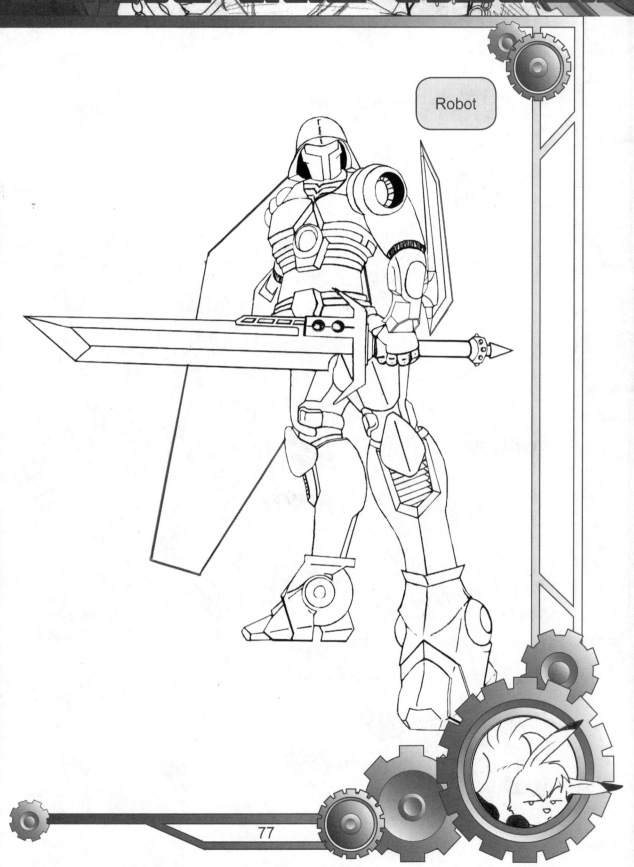

Robot

Cyber or Futuristic Characters

Magic Users, Fighters, and Warriors

Magi, wizards, witches, warlocks, sorcerers—whatever you wish to call them—all use magic. Magic users do not normally wear metal armor and typically not even leather, so they have to make do with cloth robes or other outfits. Magic users typically have either a very slim or very pudgy body type since they have to spend a lot of time studying and do not get to work their bodies as much as other people do. Magic users have a lot of accessories. They tend to have special jewelry or staves embedded with crystals to enhance their magic. Their jewelry might also have a special significance, such as their ranking in the branch of magic they are studying. Many also carry books or scrolls with them, and some have familiars. Their familiar does not have to be the standard black cat, but can be whatever would be most fitting for your character. Temperament and personalities can range from arrogant, overconfident jerks to powerful yet kind healers. This type of character is malleable to almost any situation or personality you would like to put him or her into.

The difference between fighters and warriors is quite significant. A fighter is someone who has not necessarily received formal combat training, whereas a warrior is highly trained, sometimes specializing in a very specific area of combat. Fighters and warriors cover a broad range of people who sometimes don't have anything in common other than the ability and skill to fight. Their body types usually range from heavily muscled to athletic. Ranged fighters like archers or sharpshooters tend to have a more slender but still very athletic body.

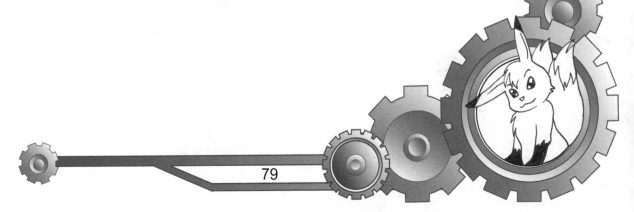

CHAPTER 3

Sorcerers can channel magic.

Sorcerer

Really more of an entertainer, a magician relies on sleight of hand.

Magician

The word "witch" has had many different connotations throughout history. Our example of an archetypal witch is more of a hedgewitch who uses nature-based magic.

Witch

These demigods are recognized for their superhuman capabilities.

Deity

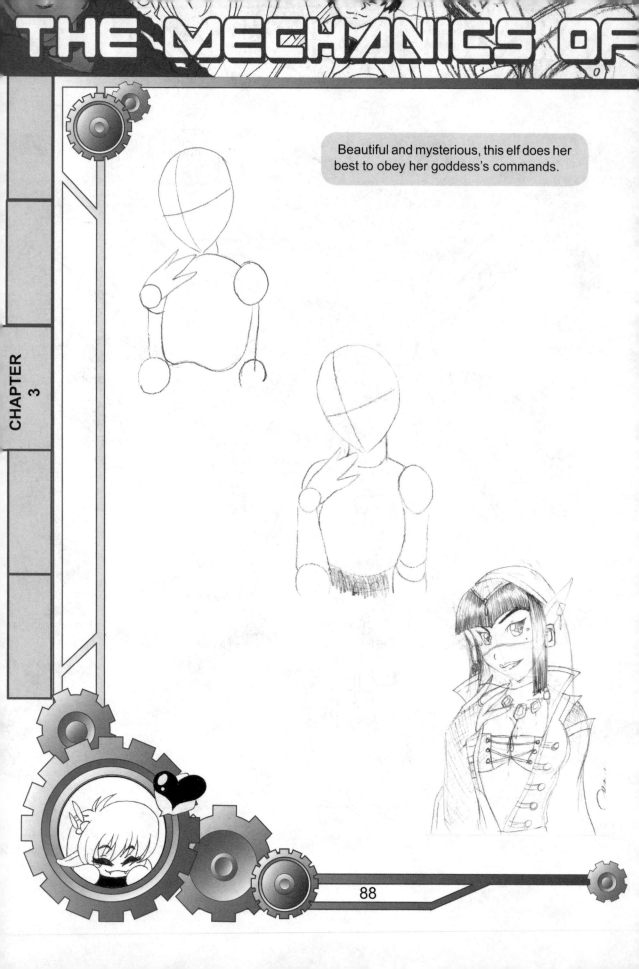

Beautiful and mysterious, this elf does her best to obey her goddess's commands.

CHAPTER 3

Elven Priestess

The ultimate woodsman, he relies heavily on his bow.

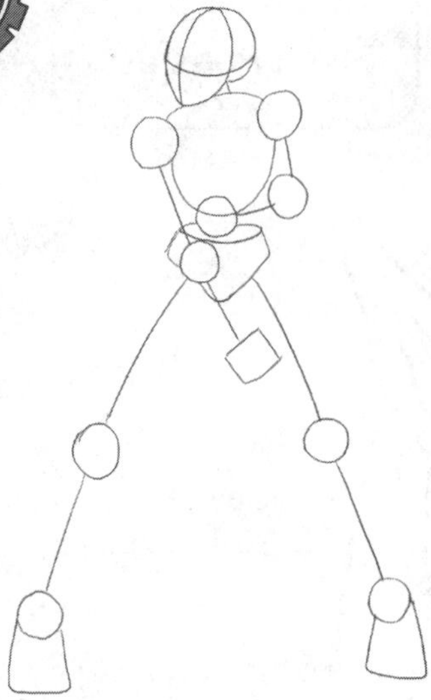

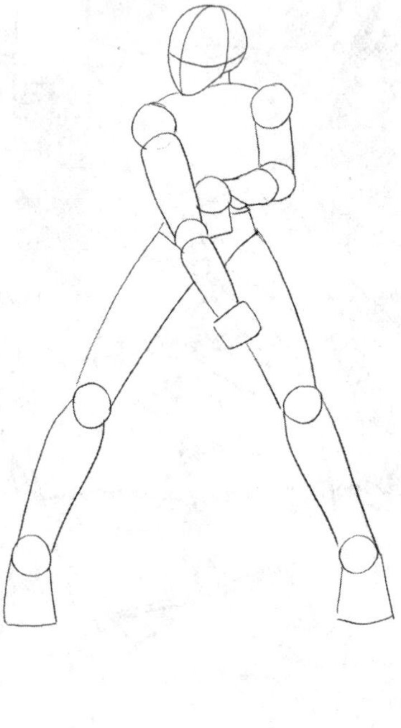

Elven Ranger

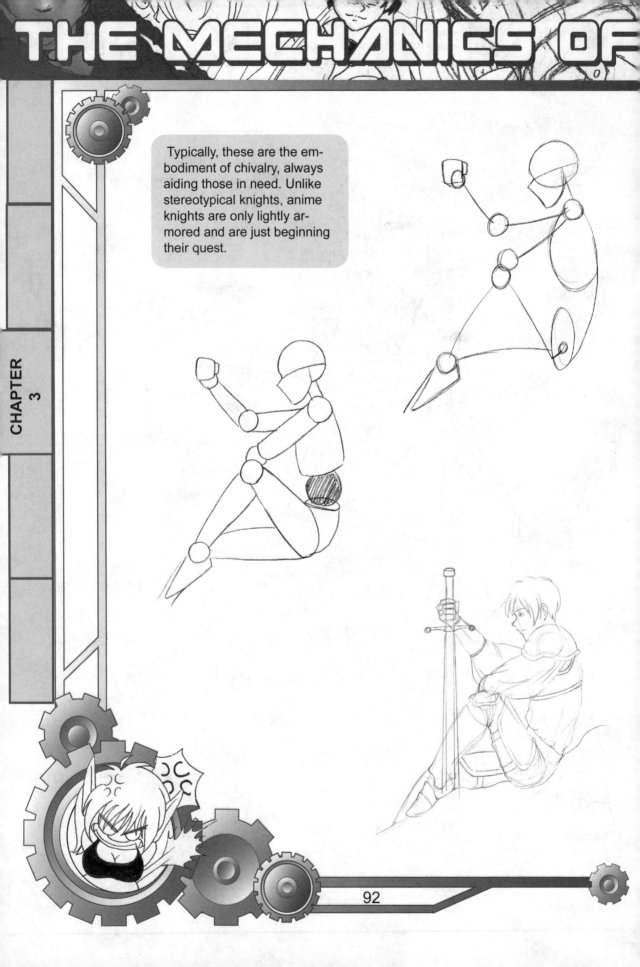

Typically, these are the embodiment of chivalry, always aiding those in need. Unlike stereotypical knights, anime knights are only lightly armored and are just beginning their quest.

Knight

Samurai were ancient Japanese warriors. Like medieval European knights, were the symbols of virtue in their culture, but as Ronin (wandering samurai)

Ronin

This is a traditional armored outfit of the samurai.

Armored Samurai

Ninjas specialize in stealth and assassination.

Traditional Ninja

Despite outrageous costuming, loud colors, and even louder attitudes, these ninjas make their way through a story based more on a saving virtue than any one ninja skill.

Fantasy Ninja

As highly skilled in stealth and assassination as their traditional predecessors, these ninjas use technology to their advantage. They make full use of things like night vision and light armor.

Futuristic Ninja

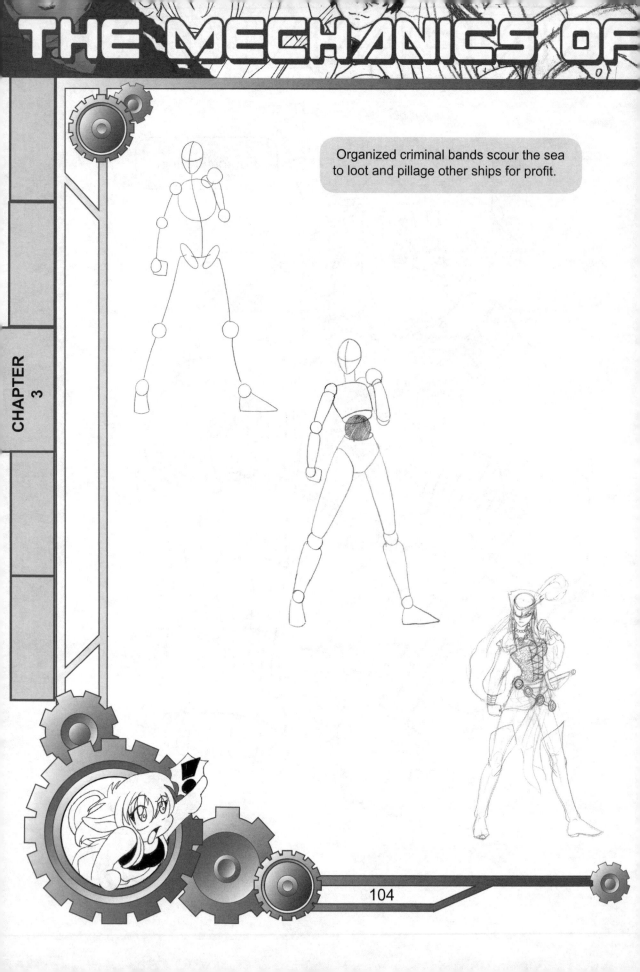

CHAPTER 3

Organized criminal bands scour the sea to loot and pillage other ships for profit.

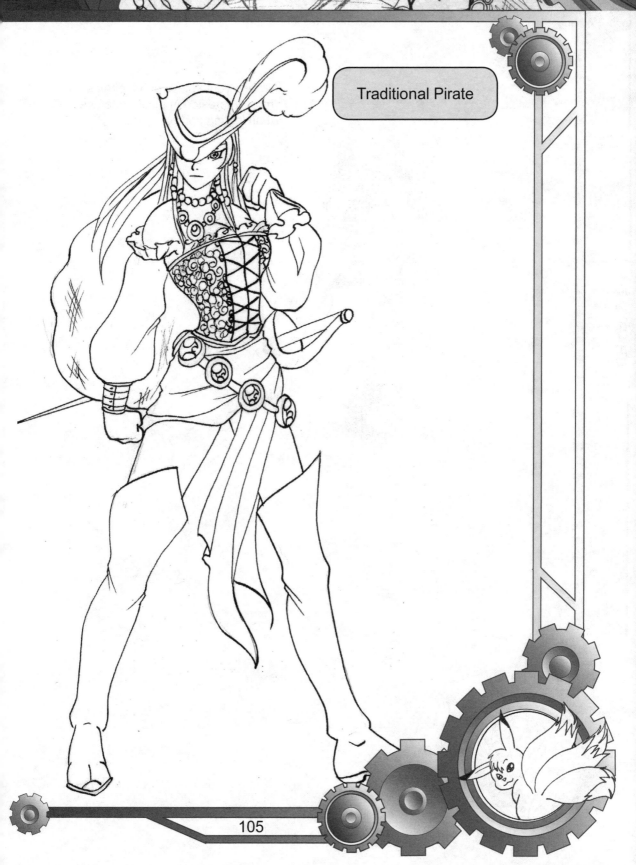

Traditional Pirate

These youthful, vigorous pirates are more interested in buried treasure than looting and pillaging.

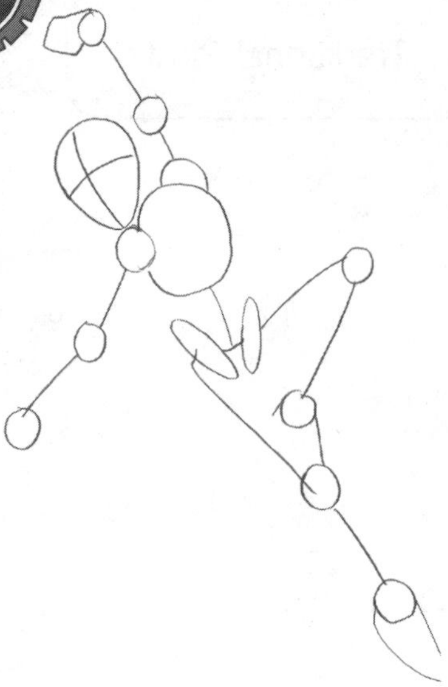

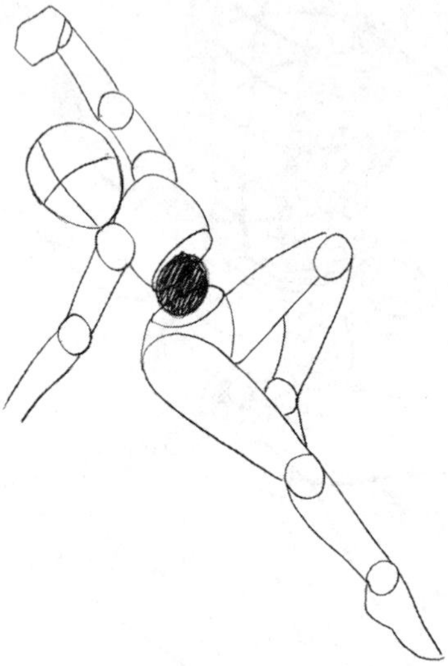

Fantasy Pirate

Although these pirates are rarely on sea ships, they loot and pillage about the same as their sea-bound counterparts. They make perfect charismatic antiheroes.

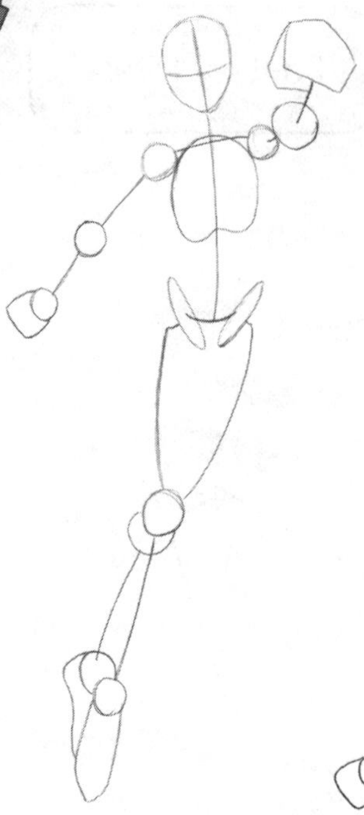

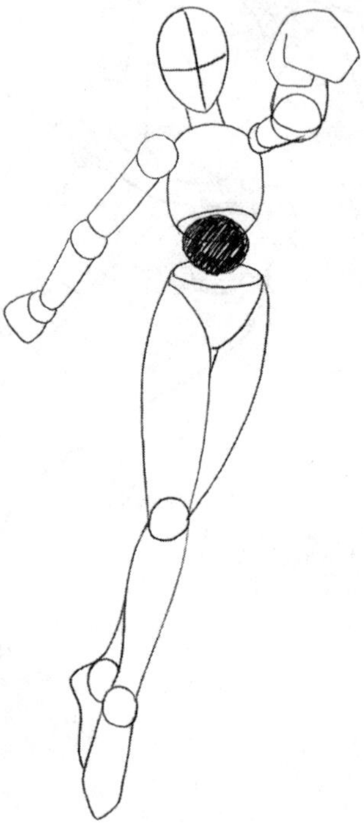

Futuristic Pirate

THE MECHANICS OF

Street fighters have built their reputations and pride on their fighting skills.

Street Fighter

Young, informally trained, and ill informed, these fighters still manage to become an integral force in the conflict.

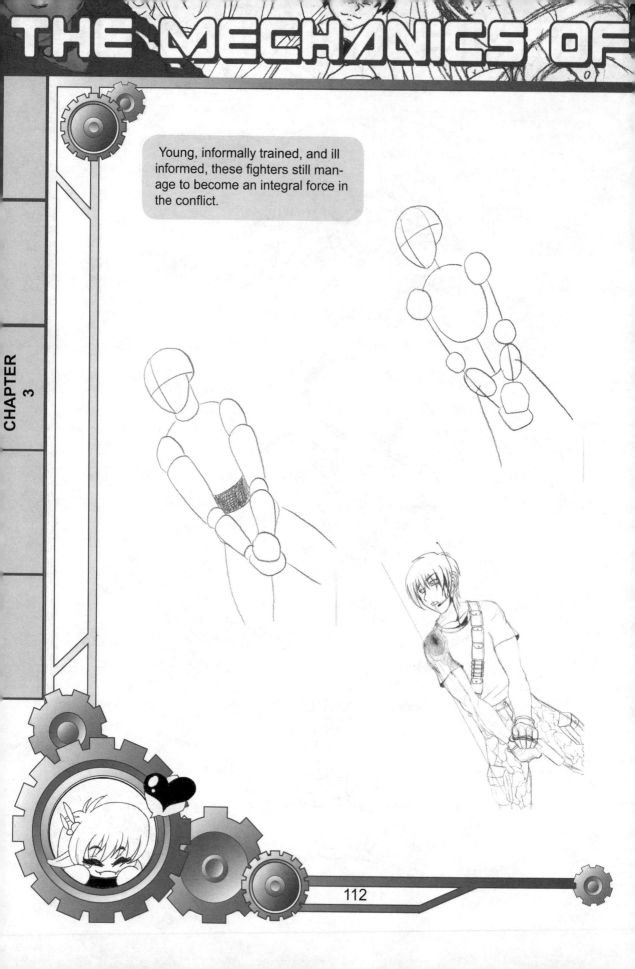

Militia/Rebel Fighter

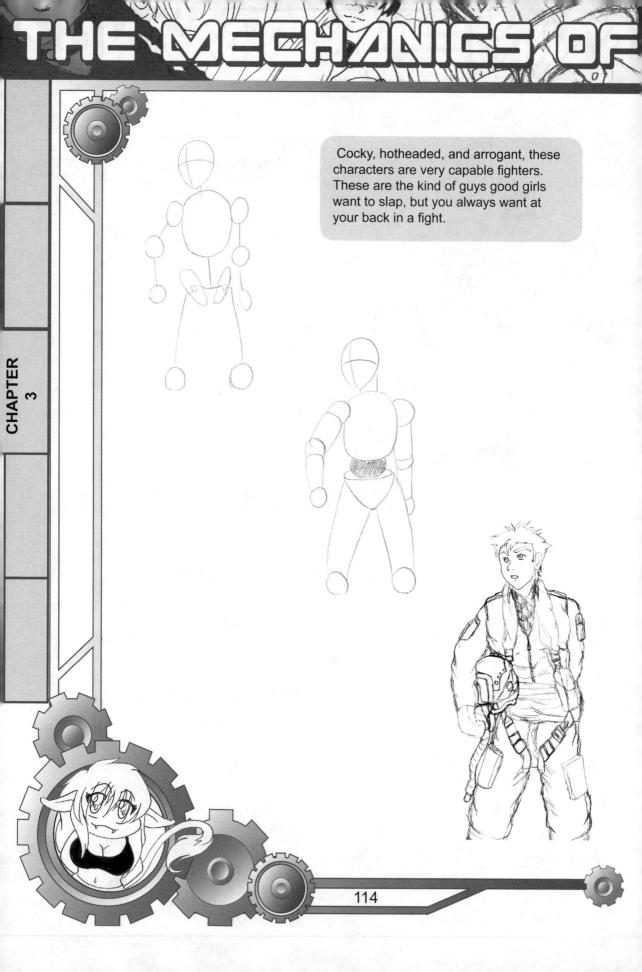

Cocky, hotheaded, and arrogant, these characters are very capable fighters. These are the kind of guys good girls want to slap, but you always want at your back in a fight.

Modern Pilot

A rogue pilot will always do what is right and honorable, but in her time, in her way, and at her leisure.

Rogue Pilot

Similar to the modern pilot but with better toys. Think transformable vessel, bigger, badder gun, etc.

Futuristic Pilot

These fighters battle on the Internet using bits of binary data for weapons. They fight in a virtual world with virtual manifestations of themselves.

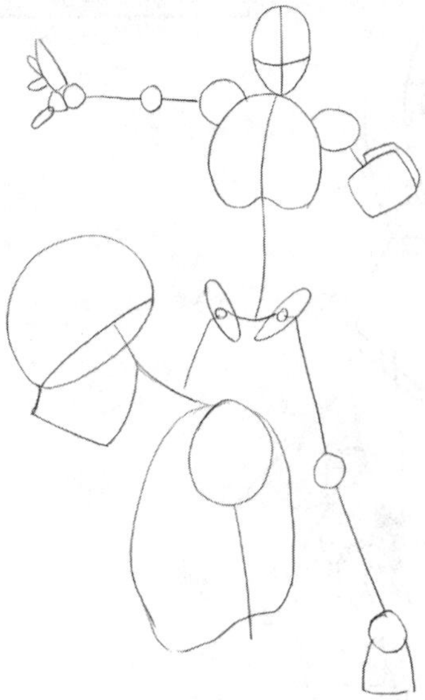

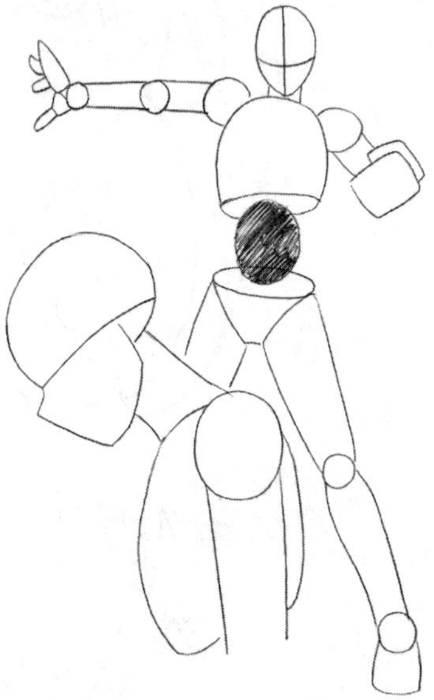

Cyber Warrior

THE MECHANICS OF

Magic Users, Fighters, and Warriors

Cat Girls and Dog Boys

Cat girls and dog boys are a general stereotype in anime. A feline humanoid does not necessarily have to be female, just as a canine humanoid does not have to be male.

In general, animalistic humanoids tend to relate very closely to the animals they are. For example, a leopard girl will love taking naps, whereas it is very important to keep a wolf puppy active and always have plenty of chew toys on hand. They will also act more impulsively and instinctually than other characters and so may act without thinking of the consequences.

Cat people and dog people will have varying degrees of animal attributes on a humanoid figure (or vice versa, human features on an animal body). The most common cat or dog person will typically have a humanoid figure with animal ears, claws, and a tail.

Cute and excitable, these girls are almost a staple in anime. Hyperactive and sometimes devious, they are a source of constant amusement and aggravation.

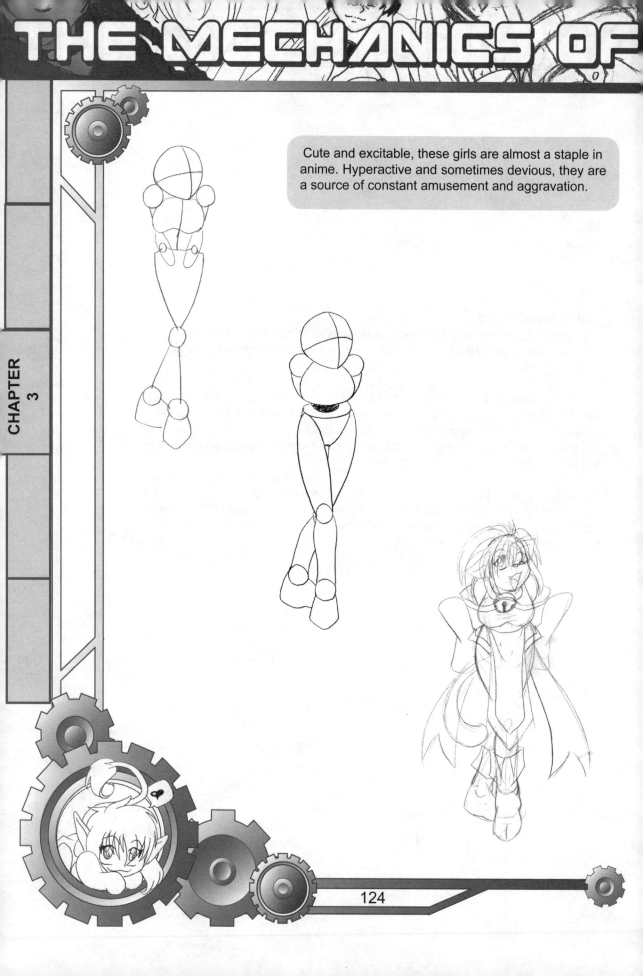

Cat Girl

CHAPTER 3

Calm and collected or loud and boisterous, they are the antithesis of cat girls. No matter the personality, they are courageous and loyal.

Dog Boy

CHAPTER 3

Cat Girl and Dog Boy

Monsters

For the purposes of this book, let's consider monsters to be non-synthetic, inhuman characters. In anime, it is not uncommon for the hero or heroine to befriend a monster in their travels. Like humans, monsters can be good guys or bad guys.

Here we give examples of youkai and oni, which are demons from Japanese mythos, as well as aliens and ghosts.

A pretty façade can hide the ugliest of spirit. Youkai have quite a bit more polish than your typical demon, but approach them with caution.

Youkai

Another Japanese demon, oni are the extreme opposite of youkai in appearance. These ogres are rough around the edges, but their gruff demeanors can sometimes hide a heart of gold.

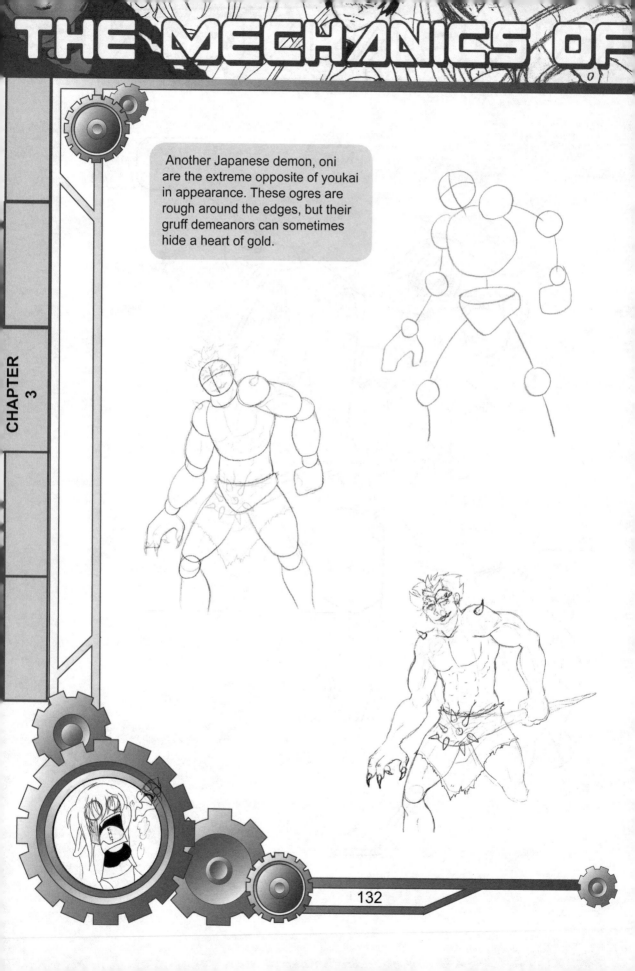

Oni

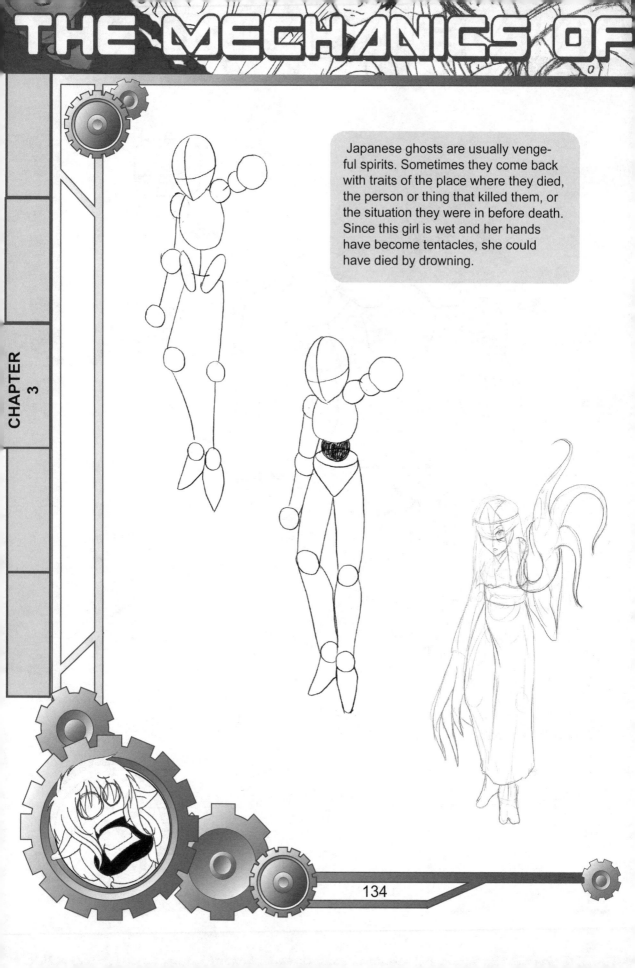

Japanese ghosts are usually vengeful spirits. Sometimes they come back with traits of the place where they died, the person or thing that killed them, or the situation they were in before death. Since this girl is wet and her hands have become tentacles, she could have died by drowning.

Ghost

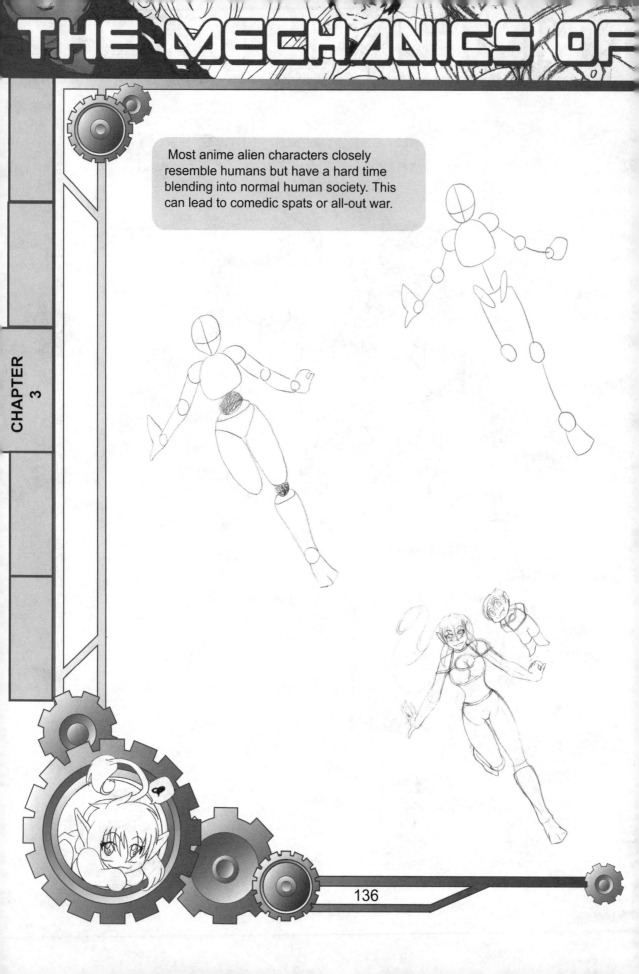

Most anime alien characters closely resemble humans but have a hard time blending into normal human society. This can lead to comedic spats or all-out war.

Alien

Monsters

Cute and Fluffy Sidekicks

You know what we're talking about. These are the creatures that make your 12-year-old cousin screech, "Awwwwwww! That's so cute!" Often useless but sometimes integral to the plot, these characters are always cute. They are designed to sell plushies, key chains, whatever you want to make in their likeness. That's why we at the studio call them the "cute marketable item."

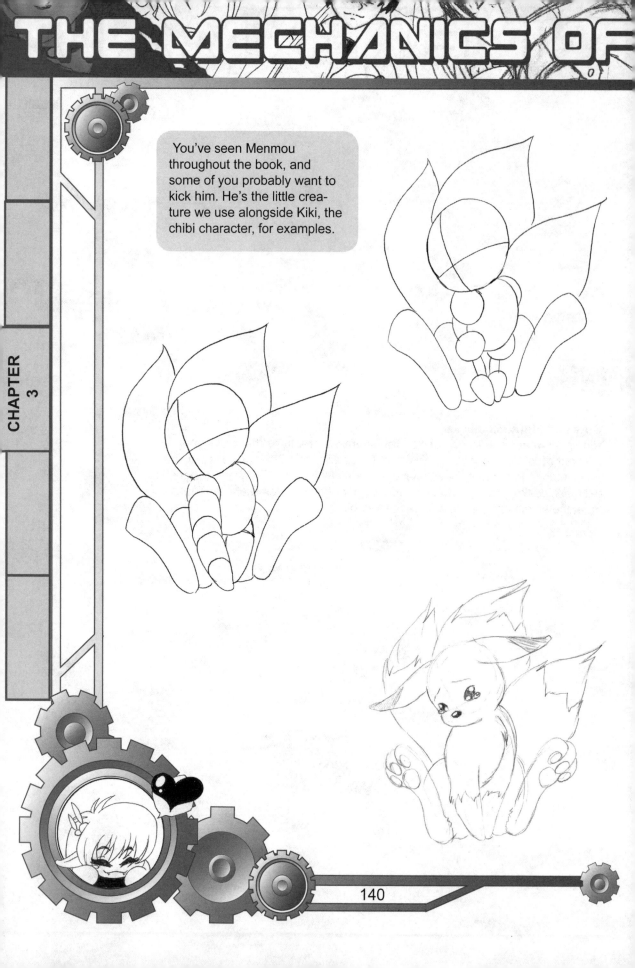

You've seen Menmou throughout the book, and some of you probably want to kick him. He's the little creature we use alongside Kiki, the chibi character, for examples.

Fluffy Sidekick

Who wouldn't want a baby dragon the size of your palm? Egg is small but very, very devious. Don't get on his bad side because he has all of your lifetime to plot his revenge against you.

Cute Pet Monster

- Creating Flow and Balance
- Ball and Stick Figures
- Translating the Figure into Basic Shapes

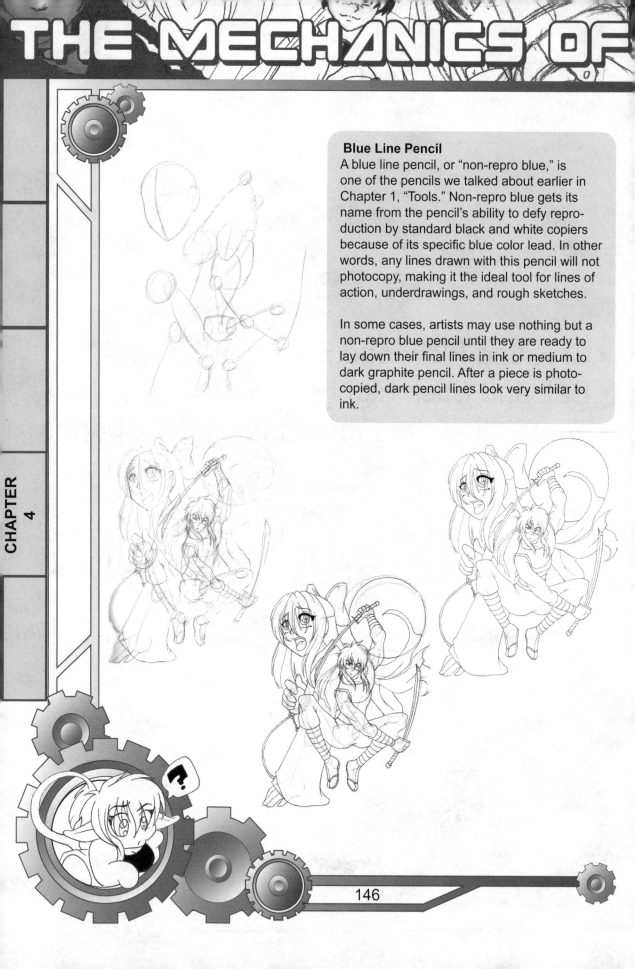

CHAPTER 4

Blue Line Pencil

A blue line pencil, or "non-repro blue," is one of the pencils we talked about earlier in Chapter 1, "Tools." Non-repro blue gets its name from the pencil's ability to defy reproduction by standard black and white copiers because of its specific blue color lead. In other words, any lines drawn with this pencil will not photocopy, making it the ideal tool for lines of action, underdrawings, and rough sketches.

In some cases, artists may use nothing but a non-repro blue pencil until they are ready to lay down their final lines in ink or medium to dark graphite pencil. After a piece is photocopied, dark pencil lines look very similar to ink.

Some artists use a non-repro blue pencil to delineate where their shadows are, especially in instances where things like screentone will be used. These techniques will be discussed later in this book.

CHAPTER 4

Creating Flow and Balance

Creating flow and balance with a body is easier said than done. One of the contributing factors for any type of character design is a sense of flow. Flow within a body is a sense of balance and movement created by its stance or placement in space. This is usually done with a "line of balance" (or "point of balance") as well as a line of movement that we refer to as a "line of action."

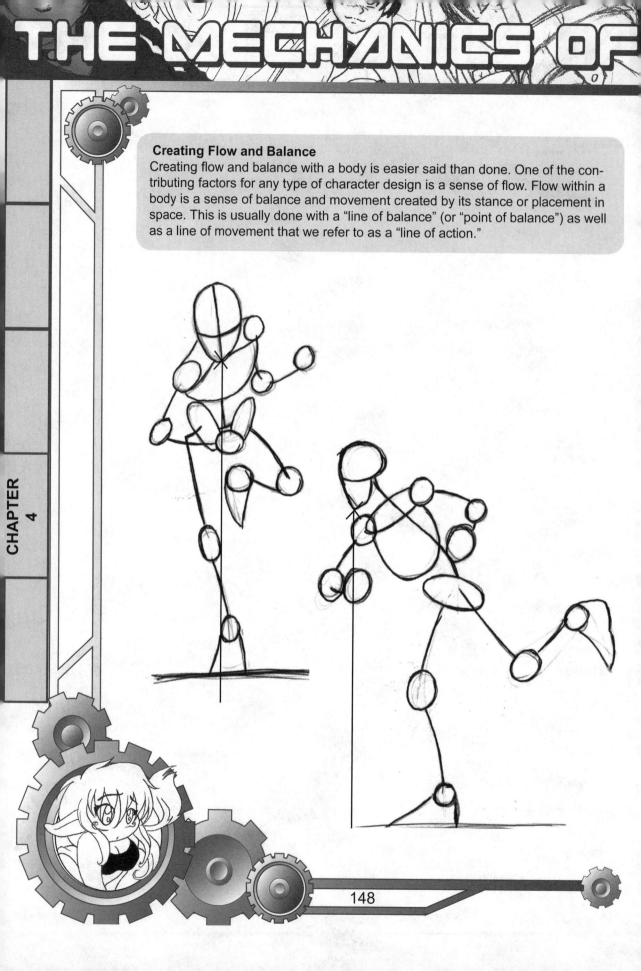

A line of action is a simple line indicating the motion of a character and where it is moving. A character with flow generally follows an "S-like" or compound curve.

On the other hand, a static character has lines of action that are relatively straight.

Even standing characters will still follow a curved line of action to avoid stiffness. Compare a stiff figure to a curved figure in the same position. Notice the difference? One character looks far more natural than the other. Remember, even in caricature/cartoon/anime form, people do not willingly stay in stiff positions.

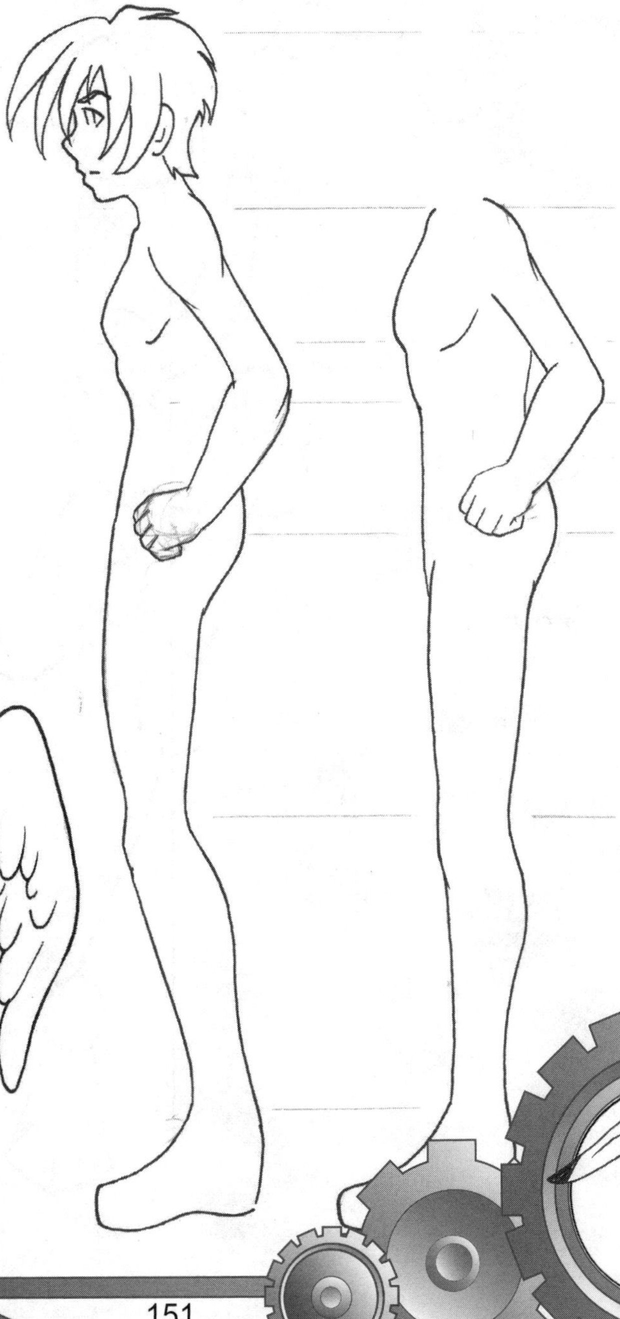

Adding balance is a little more difficult. Notice the x on this line of action. If we were to draw a line from the x to the ground, they would meet at a 90 degree angle because the character is balanced. This is also referred to as a line of balance.

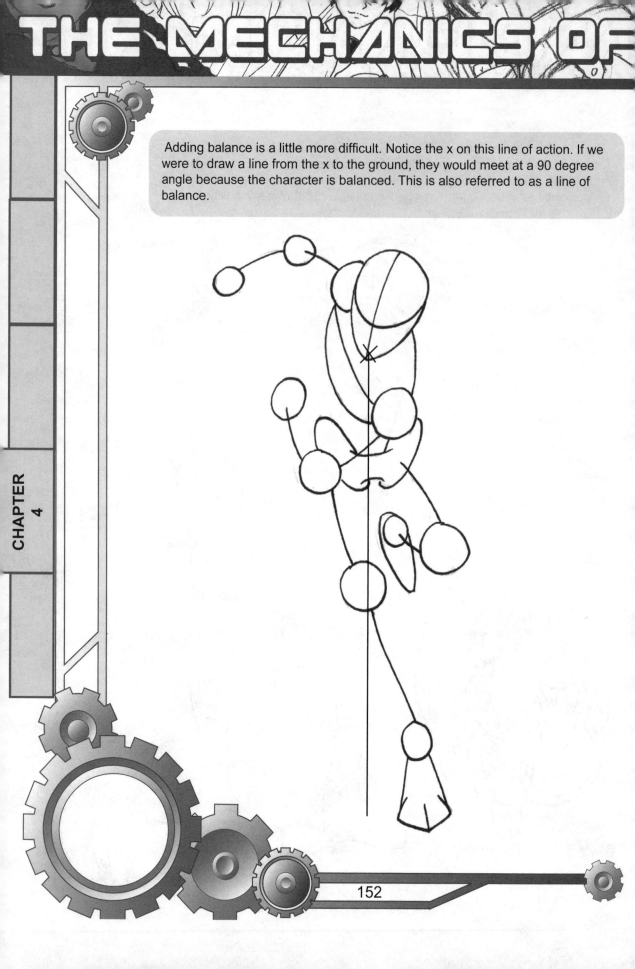

When the weight is shifted, we need something to use as a counterbalance. In this case, we gave Kiki a stack of books.

CHAPTER
4

Also, keep in mind that swimming or flying creatures almost never follow a straight line of action. They will appear to bend the traditional laws of balance and will also follow more exaggerated and complex "S" curves in their lines of action.

CHAPTER
4

Try drawing good lines of action with a non-repro blue pencil. They don't need to be anything very complex, just enough to get a good feel for a character's flow.

Check over your sketches and see how many lines have stayed balanced. Remember that when the floor plane shifts, so should the balance point. So if your character is going uphill...

...or downhill, watch out for its balance.

Here are a few characters with good lines of action...

Ball and Stick Figures

Ball and stick figures, matchstick men, simple models—these are all terms that refer to the basic line and ball joint models that are laid over the line of action. Ball and stick figures give an artist an idea of the positioning and perspective applied to a character. Circles are drawn to represent joints. Joints closer to the viewer in space are larger. This drawing is the first time we have shown perspective.

Think of the ball and stick figure as your character's skeleton. Without it, the base of your character's body could easily end up skewed or out of proportion.

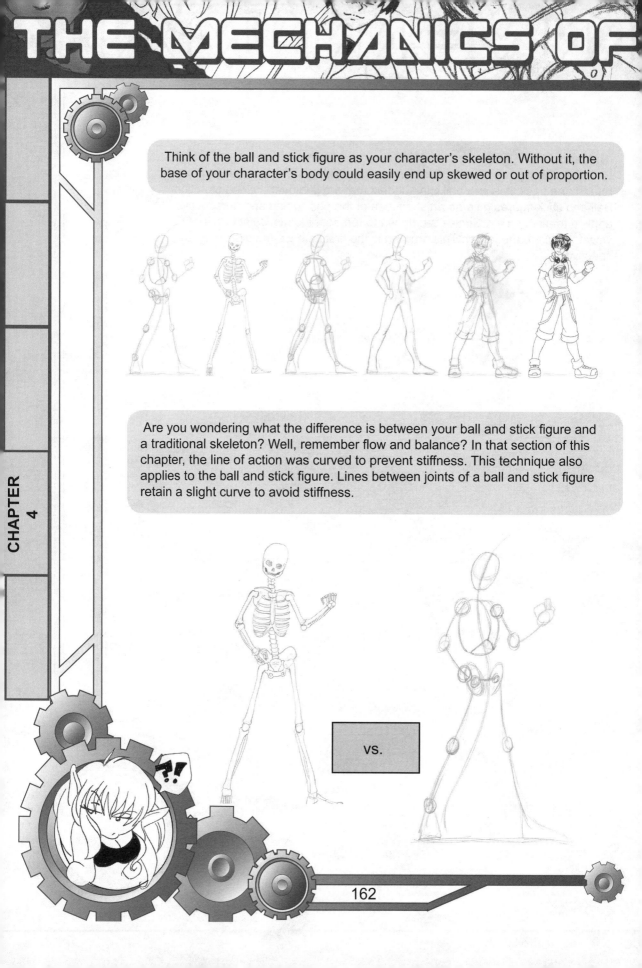

Are you wondering what the difference is between your ball and stick figure and a traditional skeleton? Well, remember flow and balance? In that section of this chapter, the line of action was curved to prevent stiffness. This technique also applies to the ball and stick figure. Lines between joints of a ball and stick figure retain a slight curve to avoid stiffness.

VS.

Here comes the tricky part. While the stick appendages need to bend, they cannot bend too far without giving a character the look of being made of goo.

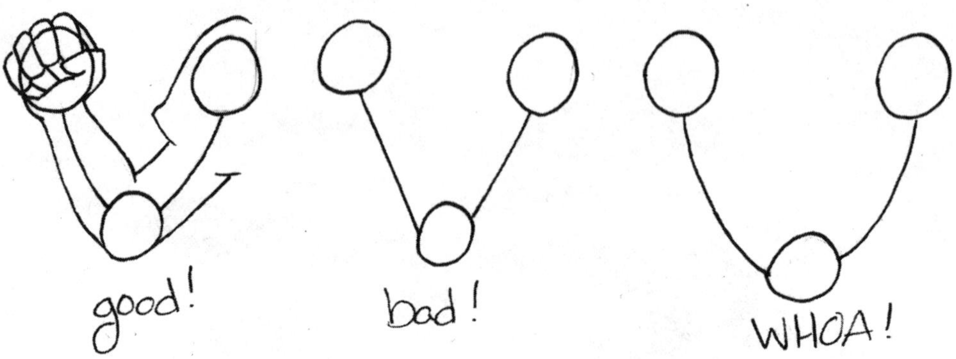

good!

bad!

WHOA!

Ball and stick figures with bends in their limbs that still follow the original line of action have a greater sense of drama and urgency than a stick figure based solely on straight lines.

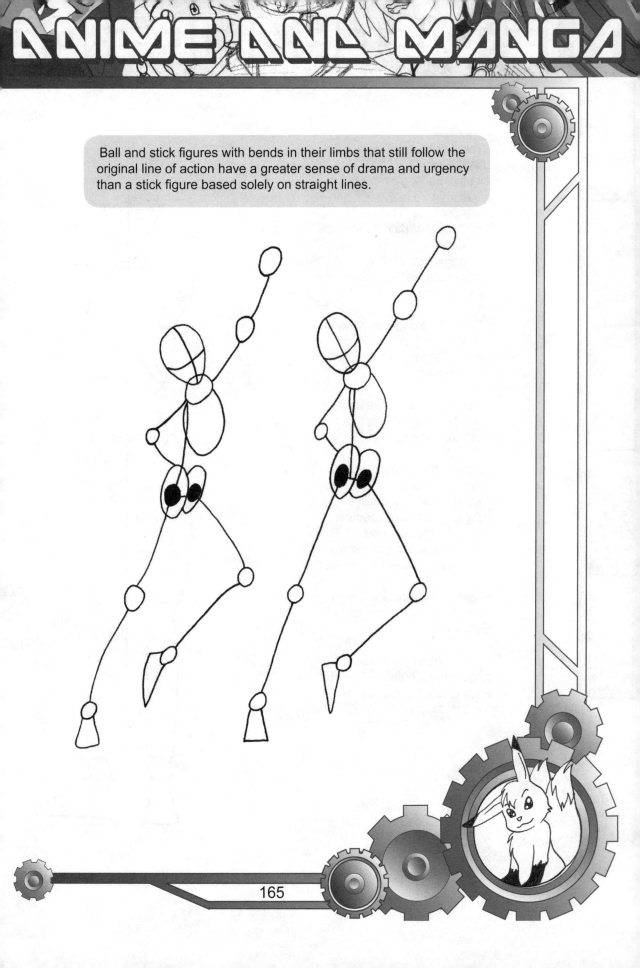

Translating the Figure into Basic Shapes

A basic drawing exercise is to break a figure into basic geometric shapes. This can help a novice artist gain confidence in illustrating a complicated figure. Here is a basic breakdown of simple shapes we apply to a humanoid figure:

• Head: An elongated sphere with a rectangular prism on the front represents the cranium and jaw.

• Neck: This looks like a short cylinder that connects the head to the torso.

• Upper chest: An ellipse will embody the chest. For heavily muscled males, the ellipse will be larger and could become more of a rhombus depending on the character. For females, the ellipse is generally smaller.

• Stomach: An oval will represent the space for the stomach.

• Pelvis: A female's pelvis is larger than a male's. Keep this in mind when you draw the tilted cube.

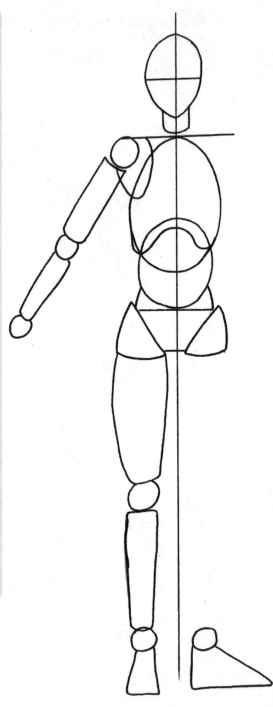

• Hips: A female's hips are larger than a male's. Use a pyramid to represent the hips.

• Thighs: Thighs are large, tapered cylinders. Depending on how muscular your character is, the pair of cylinders can be larger or smaller.

• Lower legs: These tapered cylinders are smaller than the thigh cylinders.

• Feet: Wedges represent feet. Depending on the position of a foot, use one large wedge or several smaller ones.

• Upper arms: Use cylinders, making them larger for muscular males.

• Lower arms: Use slightly tapered cylinders.

• Joints: Spheres depict all joints, including the elbows and knees.

• Hands: The hands are kind of tricky. Depending on the positioning of the hands and the relative size of the overall image, you may or may not have to go into a lot of detail on the hand. In case you do:

  • Palm: The palm is split into triangular wedges.

  • Fingers: Use tubes to connect to spheres to represent bones and joints, respectively.

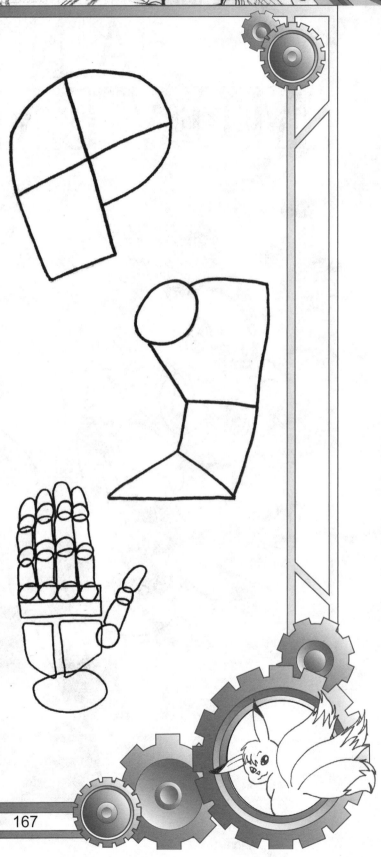

POSING AND MOVEMENT

5

- Line of Action
- Dynamic Stances
- Dramatic Poses
- Glamour Poses
- Action vs. Static Scenes

Posing and Movement

What goes on in a scene? Is your character bracing for an attack, digging a ditch, cooking dinner, preparing to cast a spell, or arguing with a friend? How you arrange a character to convey these actions is very important for a viewer's interest level. It's very boring to stare at a talking head. Besides, showing your character moving around and doing random little things helps to convey personality and background. A sweet little schoolgirl might bustle around her home preparing an extravagant meal for a picnic with friends. A warrior might polish his sword as he discusses news with his squire. Have them do something, anything!

Line of Action

Lines of action were covered in Chapter 4, "Blue Line Pencil." Recall that a good line of action is the basis of any pose. Remember flow and balance? It all starts with line of action. For the sake of poses, a line of action is your backbone and should never be taken for granted.

Dynamic Stances

Dynamic stances, or action poses, are high movement, high tension, and high excitement poses. They are the meat and potatoes of an action scene. Dynamic poses embody the high-flying kick of a martial artist, the comical handstand of a jester, and the twisting single handstand of a break-dancer. Sharply opposing angles in the body and radically conversed direction in limbs characterize these poses. Many times dynamic poses feature arms or legs thrown away from or toward the body at a harsh or extreme angle.

This scene is of an elven warrior in the middle of fighting with an enemy.

CHAPTER 5

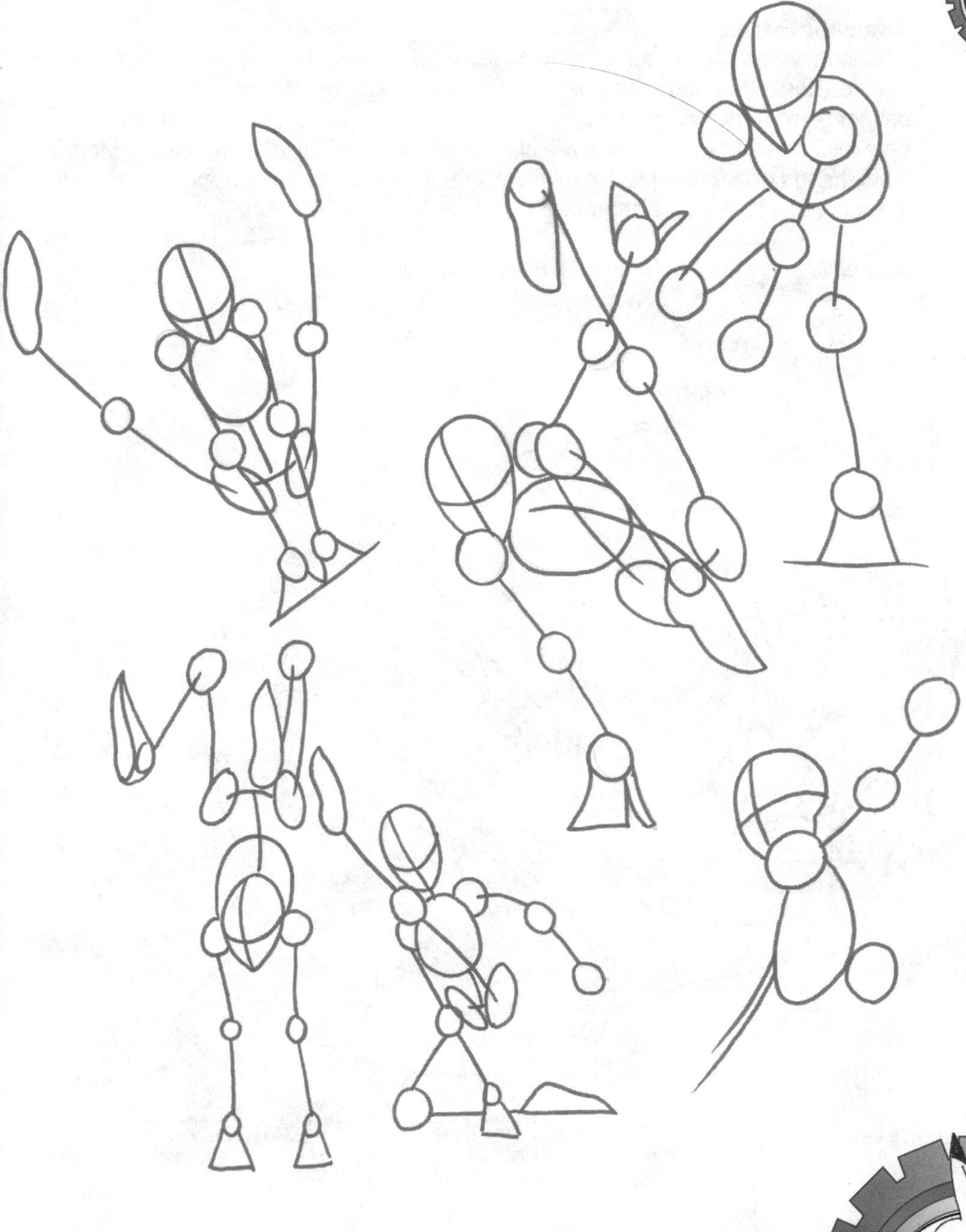

Dramatic Poses

Dramatic poses are not necessarily high movement poses, but rather poses of high tension. Dramatic poses usually embody the grace of magic casting, the pain of a fist clenching in anger, or the flippant flick of a wrist as a character orders his drink. Dramatic poses are characterized by wildly differing depth. Many times hands or feet are placed much farther in the foreground or much farther in the background than the character's body or face.

This elf is in a magic duel and is about to unleash a spell.

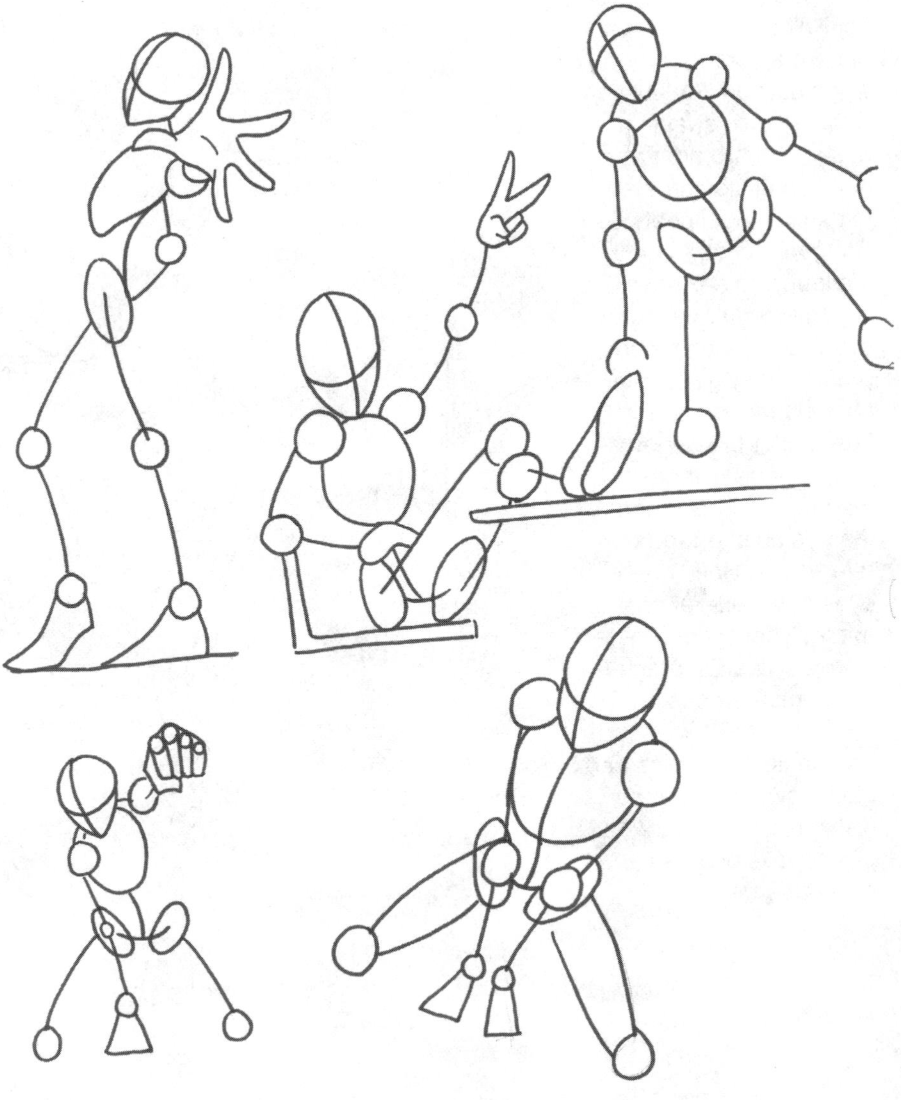

Glamour Poses

Glamour poses are sexy, posed, and rarely comfortable. These poses stick out like a sore thumb when used in conjunction with dynamic or action poses, but are right at home in pieces created to mimic model shots. Glamour poses embody the lounging sexiness of a lingerie model, the sultry spunk of a jeans model, or the smoky gaze of a makeup model. These poses litter the pages of ads, especially in fashion magazines. This means there is no shortage of references. Half-lidded eyes or severe, almost unnaturally tense limbs even when reclined characterize glamour poses.

The angle of her hips and the tension in her arms distinguish this character's provocative pose as a glamour shot.

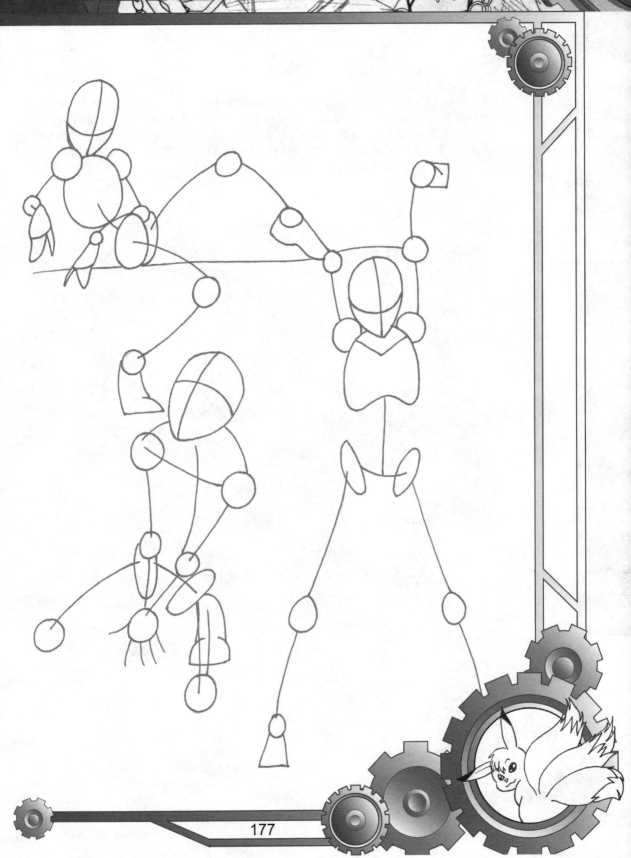

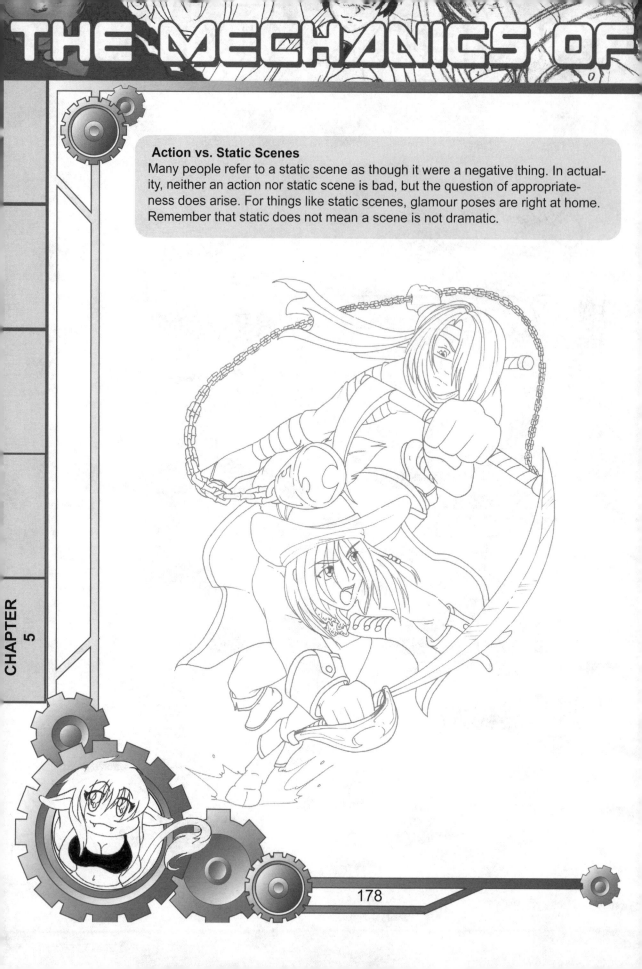

Action vs. Static Scenes

Many people refer to a static scene as though it were a negative thing. In actuality, neither an action nor static scene is bad, but the question of appropriateness does arise. For things like static scenes, glamour poses are right at home. Remember that static does not mean a scene is not dramatic.

CHAPTER 5

Though action scenes are certainly more eye catching, they can hurt the development of both characters and plot. If every panel in a comic were an action scene, both characters and stories would go flat. Remember that an action scene is a quick eye-catcher, but not necessarily a fix-all for a plot.

BASIC BODY SPECS

6

- Anime's Basic Builds
  - Muscular/Idol
  - Athletic
  - Average
  - Skinny
  - Cartoon/Simplistic
- Heads
  - Faces
  - Eyes
  - Expressions
  - Hair
- Torso   • Arms   • Hands
- Legs   • Feet

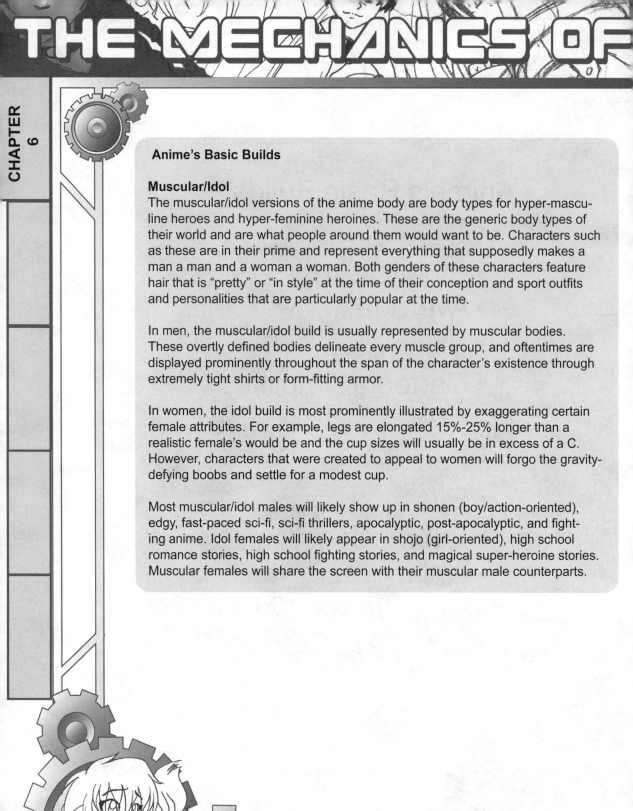

Anime's Basic Builds

Muscular/Idol

The muscular/idol versions of the anime body are body types for hyper-masculine heroes and hyper-feminine heroines. These are the generic body types of their world and are what people around them would want to be. Characters such as these are in their prime and represent everything that supposedly makes a man a man and a woman a woman. Both genders of these characters feature hair that is "pretty" or "in style" at the time of their conception and sport outfits and personalities that are particularly popular at the time.

In men, the muscular/idol build is usually represented by muscular bodies. These overtly defined bodies delineate every muscle group, and oftentimes are displayed prominently throughout the span of the character's existence through extremely tight shirts or form-fitting armor.

In women, the idol build is most prominently illustrated by exaggerating certain female attributes. For example, legs are elongated 15%-25% longer than a realistic female's would be and the cup sizes will usually be in excess of a C. However, characters that were created to appeal to women will forgo the gravity-defying boobs and settle for a modest cup.

Most muscular/idol males will likely show up in shonen (boy/action-oriented), edgy, fast-paced sci-fi, sci-fi thrillers, apocalyptic, post-apocalyptic, and fighting anime. Idol females will likely appear in shojo (girl-oriented), high school romance stories, high school fighting stories, and magical super-heroine stories. Muscular females will share the screen with their muscular male counterparts.

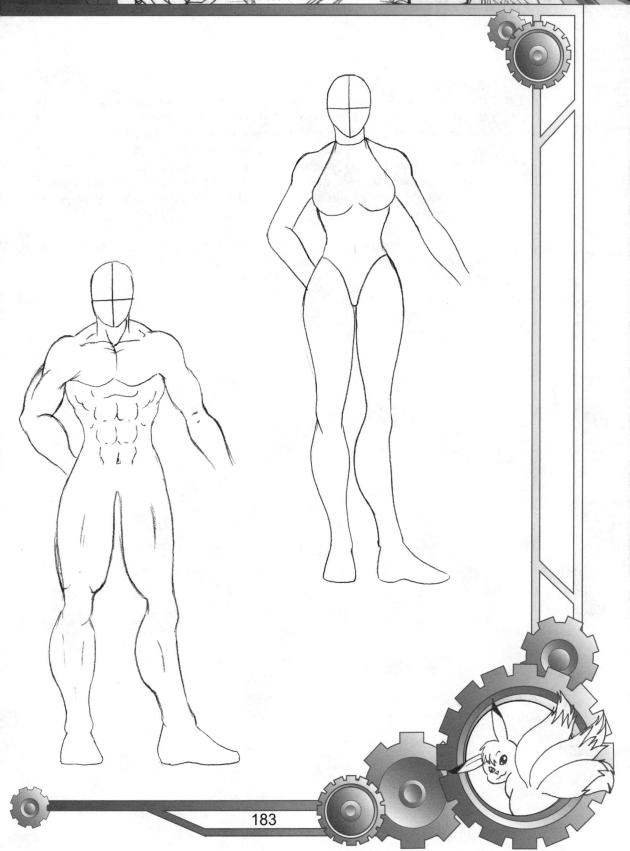

Athletic

Characters with the athletic build tend to be more realistic. Characters of this archetype are, again, in their prime, but are not as exaggerated or stereotypical as their masculine/idol counterparts. They are usually well built, soundly structured, and proportionally similar to a realistic figure. The only real difference lies in the formation of their faces. Though realistic in body structure, a character with an athletic build can still retain the wide, expressive eyes that most anime characters embody, though a male's eyes will usually be angular and less exaggerated than a female's.

Athletic characters are often used in high school fight pieces, dramas, police/action pieces, and sci-fi with political undertones and adult themes. These can be either shojo or shonen, as the story dictates.

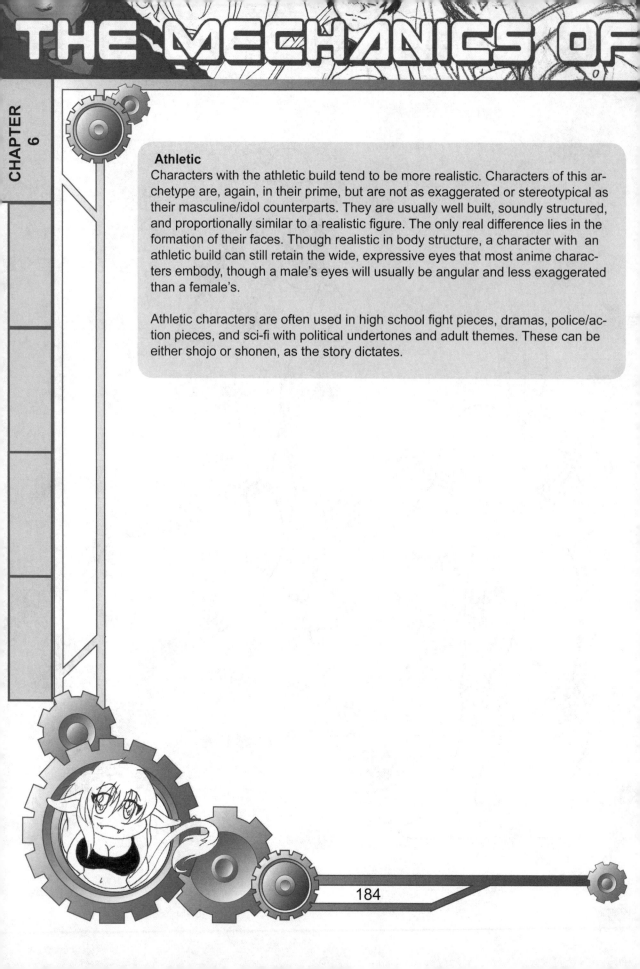

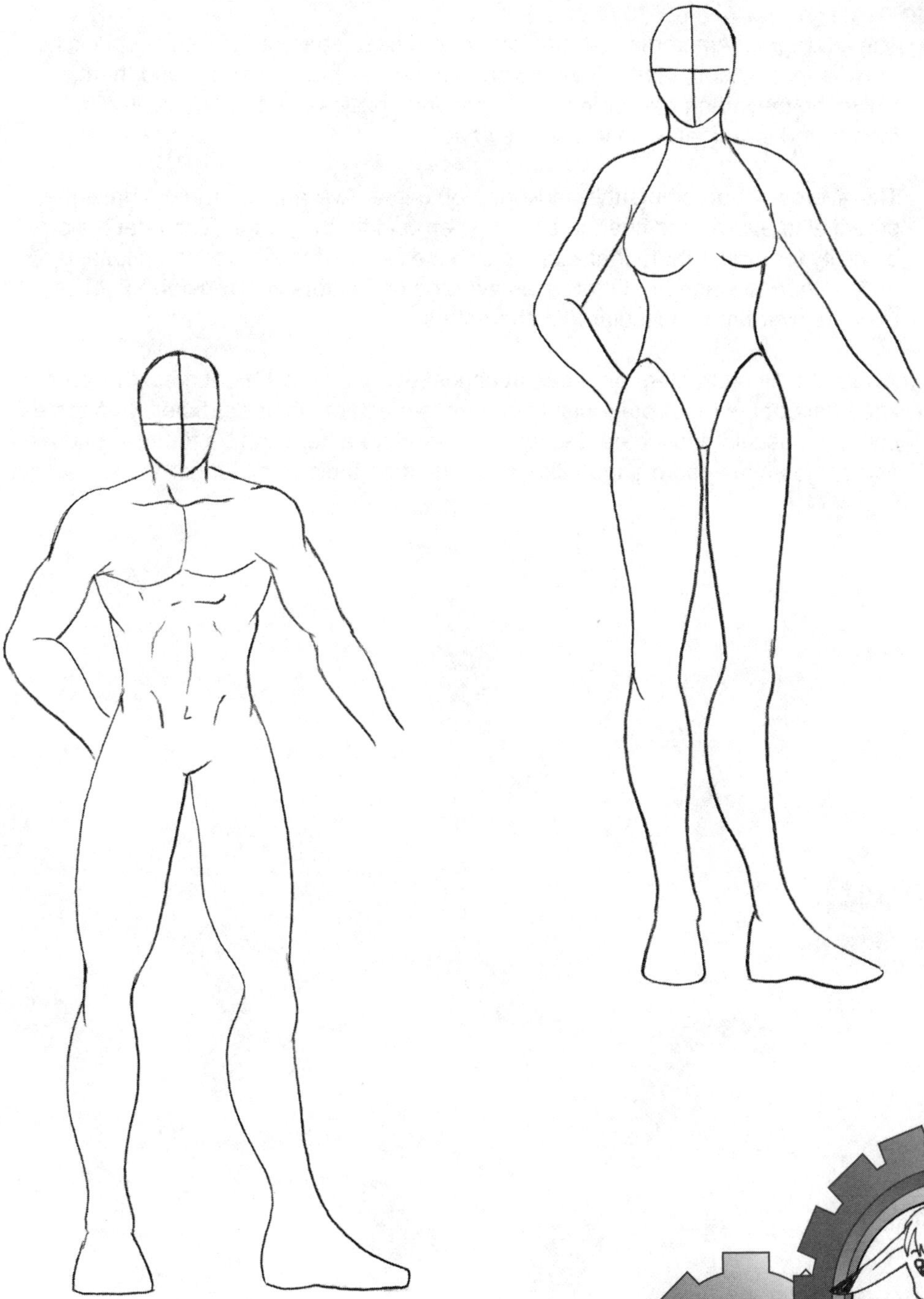

Average

The average character is just that: average. These characters aren't especially "built" and they don't have any outward differences from those around them. However, they often harbor inner powers and abilities that their muscular/idol friends and teammates only wish they had.

The average character is the backbone of anime. Average characters have the potential to evolve and change as things around them change. They have more capacity for drama than characters that have reached their max potential and have begun to stagnate. Oftentimes average characters will transform into, or become over time, muscular/idol characters.

Average built characters are seen in almost every anime. Oftentimes, the average character is the protagonist and spends much of his or her time trying to become a muscular/idol character. Again, these characters can be found in shonen and shojo anime and manga alike, depending on their core stories.

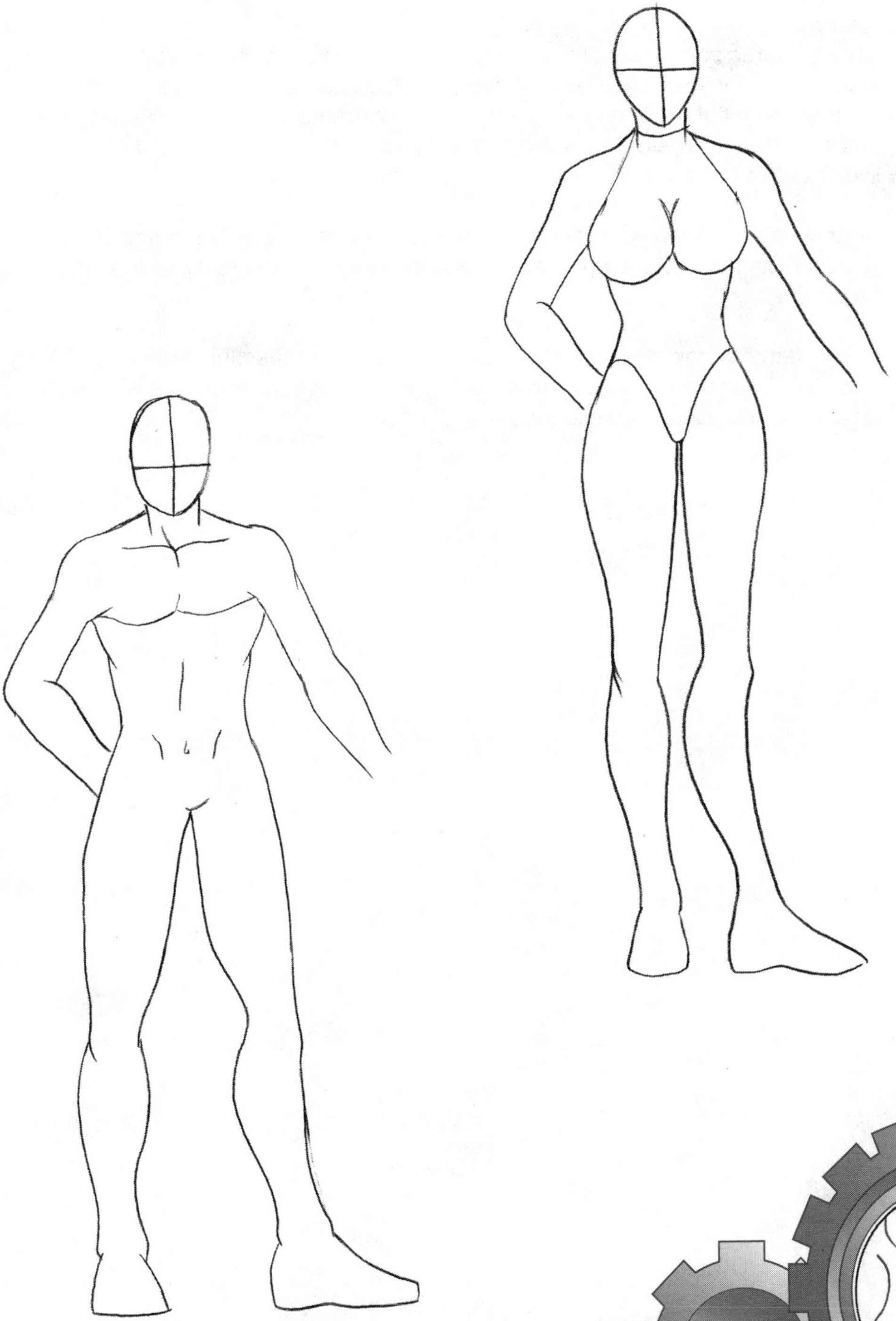

Skinny

Skinny characters are small in comparison to even their average counterparts. A skinny character is usually the most quiet and unassuming person or the loudest and most full of attitude. They are the extreme ones that drive subplots and side stories. Their stories are sad and their bodies match the wear that their lives have put on them.

Most shojo (girl-oriented) manga and anime use skinny male figures as their protagonists to offset the often muscular/idol antagonists, and these too tend to be full of angst.

Skinny females can appear just about anywhere, whereas their male counterparts tend to show up more in shojo anime and manga because of their particular appeal and use in these stories.

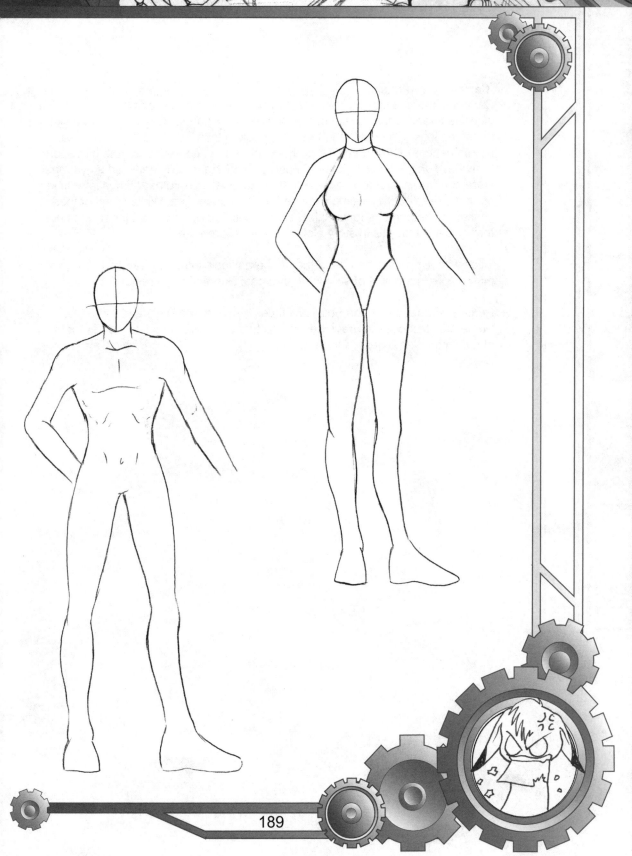

Cartoon/Simplistic

Cartoon/simplistic characters appeal to younger audiences and strike a chord in older generations that take them back to their childhood. The simple, tube-like arms and legs of these characters hark back to their Hanna-Barbera and Disney influences. They have little body structure beyond their basic elements, and likely have very little well-defined muscle. They are usually depicted as younger, more carefree characters, ones that may have fallen onto hard times later in life, or characters that have simply chosen a life of adventure. While many of these characters belong to shonen titles, shojo titles that are more lighthearted in nature and adventurous in story plot may also incorporate them.

Titles with simplistic characters tend to be episodic in nature, rarely dealing with much more in the way of subplot than a goal like "find the treasure."

Remember that these character instances are what are likely and probable. Some artists choose to draw their characters in a style completely different than others in the same genre for effect.

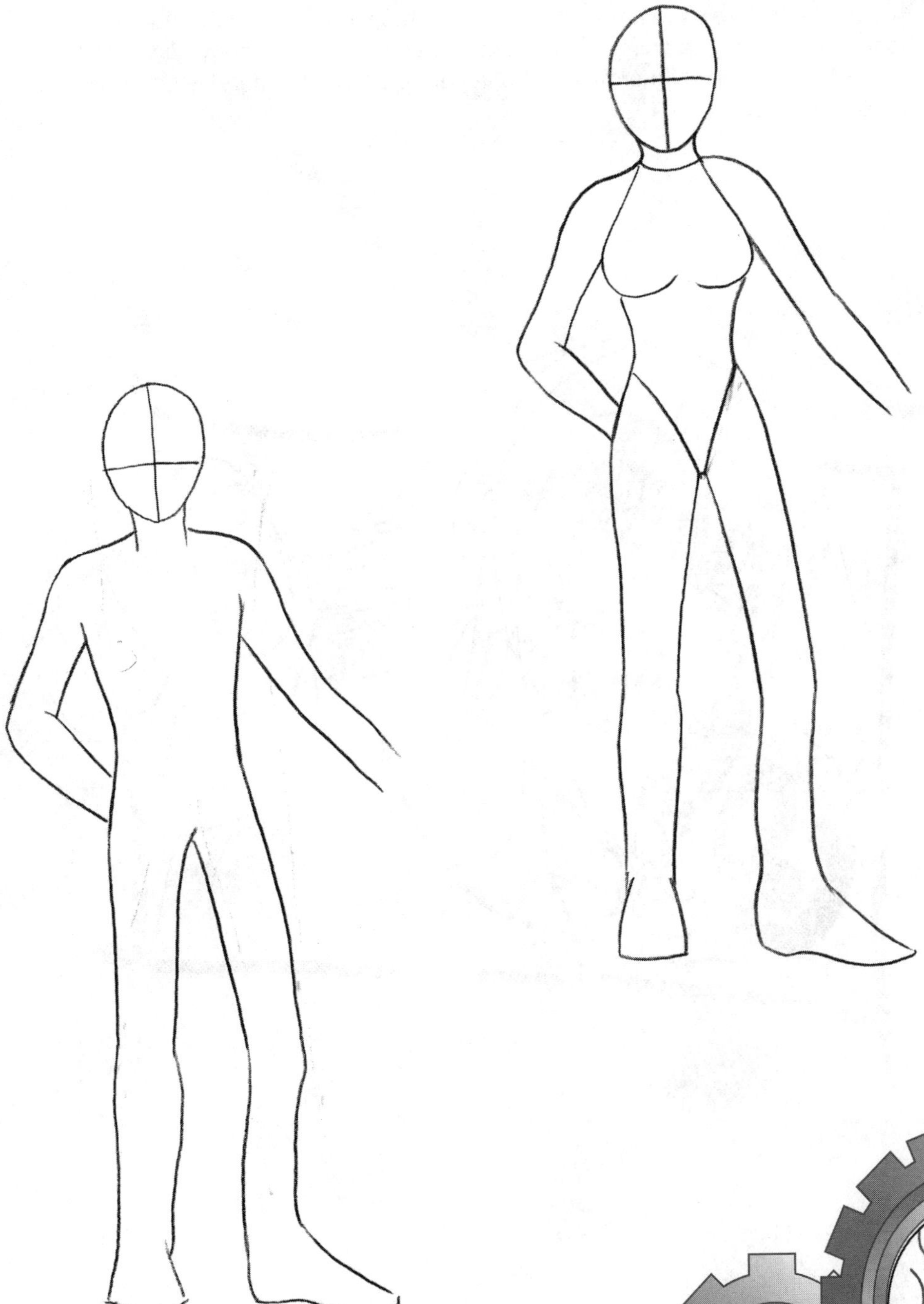

Heads

Heads are probably the hardest piece of anatomy on the human (or inhuman) body to bring into the anime style. Because so much of the body stays relatively true to the realistic style or an American cartoon style, the head is crucial to set the figure apart.

Compare the three examples below. The circular portion of the head becomes the upper cranium, while the rectangle on the front becomes the face and jaw. Sometimes the jaw is simplified all the way to a point on the front of an egg-shaped skull.

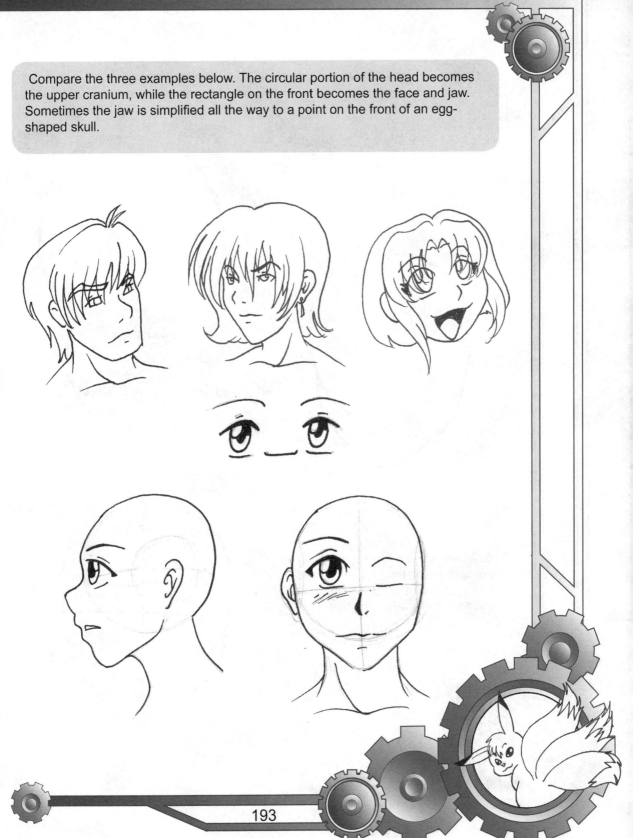

Here is an easy five-step guide to creating heads:

1. Draw a simple circle.

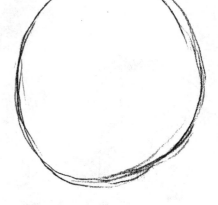

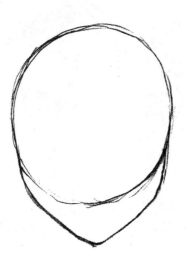

2. Add on the chin, but keep the circle lines.

3. Put cross-section guides to denote where the eyes and mouth should go. The cross-point should go in the very middle of the character's face.

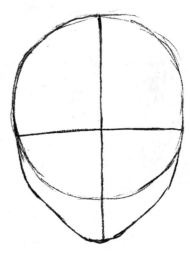

4. Add lips at the bottom of the circle, the nose near the cross-point, and ears at the horizontal guide.

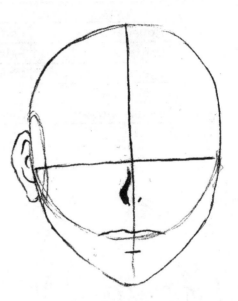

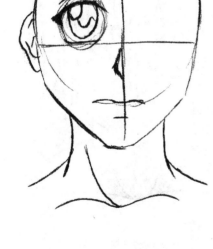

5. Draw your character's eyes. The bottom of your character's eyes should be on the horizontal guide. Put the eyelid on top of the eyeball and add eyebrows at half an eye-length above the eye. Your character's neck thickness varies by sex.

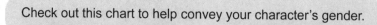

Check out this chart to help convey your character's gender.

Girls	vs.	Boys
Rounder faces		Longer faces
Larger eyes		Smaller/thinner eyes
Eyelashes		Plain eyelashes (if any)
Thin necks		Thicker necks and shoulders
Smaller noses		Defined noses

Faces

The most expressive part of the anime character is the head. As a complex joining of culturally specific expressions and universally accepted features, the anime or manga face is key to a great character. It shows the emotions of the character and displays its moods to the world. Sometimes the expression can say much more than dialogue could convey.

Here are some examples of different facial archetypes:

Cute and Perky Characters

These characters have happy expressions. They have wide, expressive mouths, thin, high eyebrows, and a small nose. Sometimes the nose is not visible. Their hairstyles tend to be a bit wild, windswept, or unkempt.

Strong-willed or Fighter Characters
Strong characters have a firmly set mouth and level eyebrows. Their hair is usually short, easily manageable, or both.

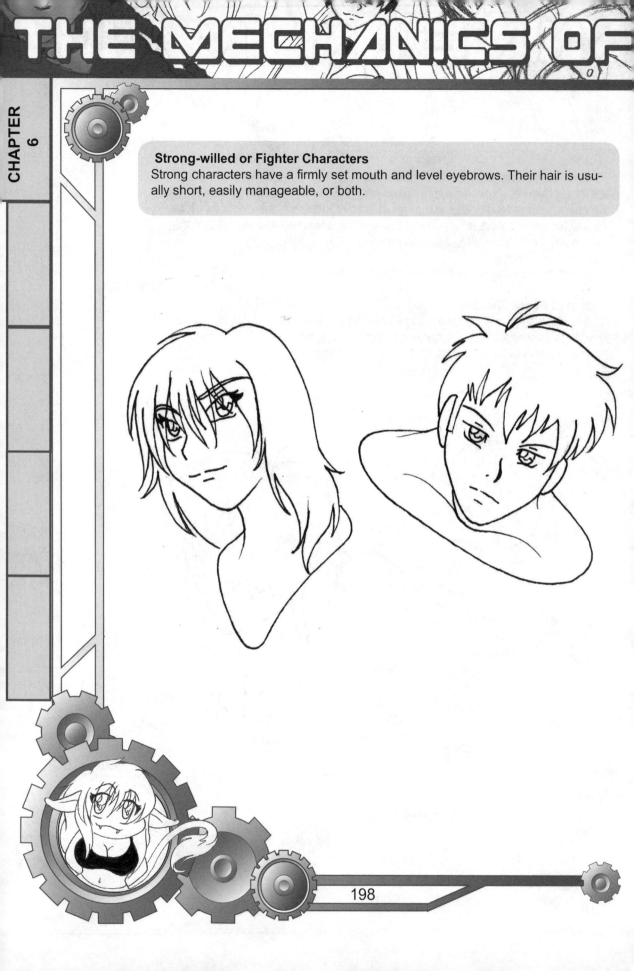

Calm, Cool, and Collected Characters

A penny for your thoughts? No. Just no. These characters keep guarded or neutral expressions even when the situation would send most screaming and crying into the night. They have straight lips that sometimes border on a frown. Their eyes are always partially obscured, usually with glasses or hair. Their hairstyles are neutral or at least orderly.

Spoiled or Selfish Characters

Think stereotypical rich person: upturned nose, one arched eyebrow, well-groomed hair, and usually looking down on someone or something. Their mouths are often in pouting or disapproving frowns.

Gentle, Happy Characters
These characters usually have smiles. Even when neutral, their mouths are just a tad upturned. Their hair is drawn in straight or sweeping lines. Their eyebrows resemble half-moons and their eyes are closed in contentment or happiness.

Weak-Willed or Nerdy Characters
Think of a very shy person. These characters don't usually look you in the eye and they keep their face averted when they can, sometimes using their bangs to hide behind. Their eyebrows are tilted downward in worry and their mouths are in anxious frowns.

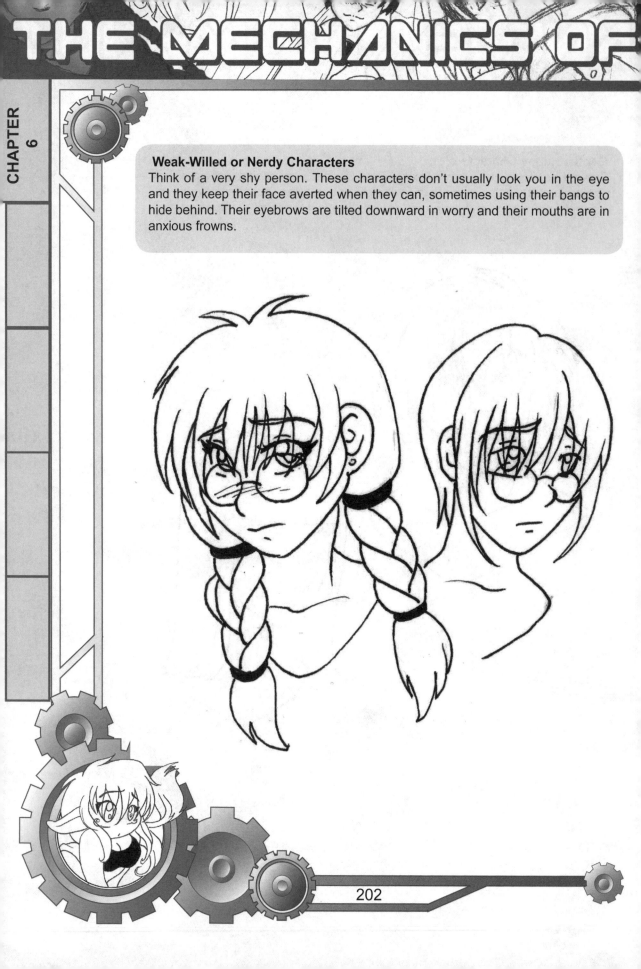

Villainous or Suspicious Characters

Spiky hair, pierced…you'd think these characters were part of the punk archetype. Their eyes are narrow, their eyebrows are furrowed in mischievous thoughts and plans, and their mouths are slightly upturned in devious smiles.

Eyes

Another feature you will have to contend with is the eyes. Anime eyes are known for their huge, expressive pupils and watery-looking irises. These ornate facets of a character are probably the most complex piece of the head. Add to this the fact that not all anime eyes are the same. In fact, some of them look very realistic at times. You will have the challenge of picking your poison, so to speak.

Large, round, watery eyes are viewed as soft and somber, reflecting peacefulness until an outside element, such as a fire in the eyes, literally, affects them. Large slanted eyes are intense, and very often reflect the inner nature of a character as being very passionate. Both sets of large eyes have a tendency to be viewed as youthful and vibrant.

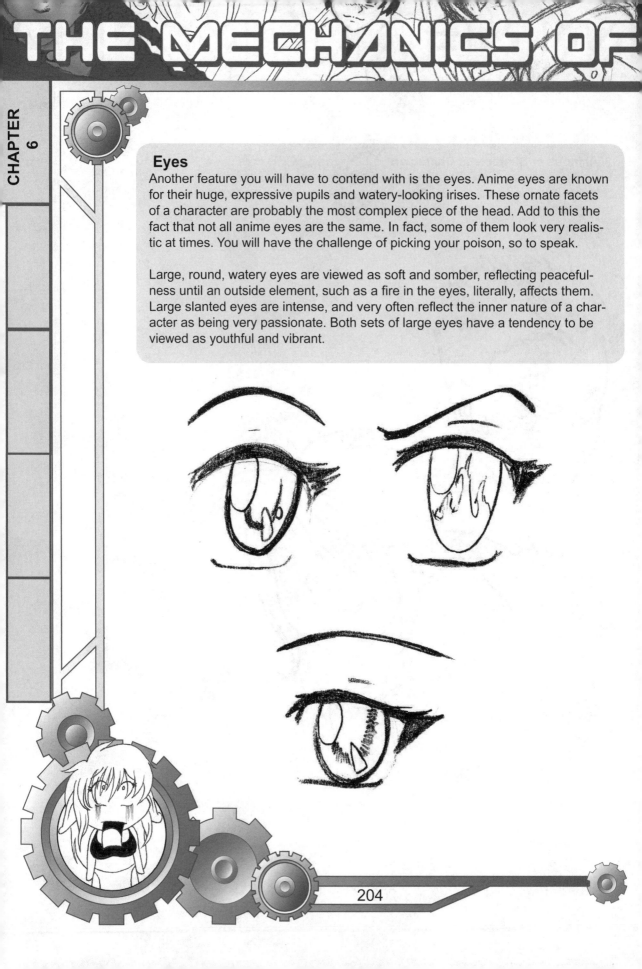

Medium-sized eyes, those closest to a "realistic" look, are the run-of-the-mill kind of eyes. They are neutral in what they say about a character until he or she is affected by an emotion. Medium-sized, slanted eyes hint at a personality that has seen more than its years, retaining the size of a youth's but gaining the look of experience. Medium-sized rounded eyes maintain more of the youthful innocence.

Smaller eyes, especially those that are slanted or squinted, hint at either a sinister intent or a shadowy personality. Characters with smaller eyes tend to be viewed as mysterious. They have a lot to hide from the world, and fully open eyes could give it all away.

The following page contains examples of anime eyes of several different shapes and sizes.

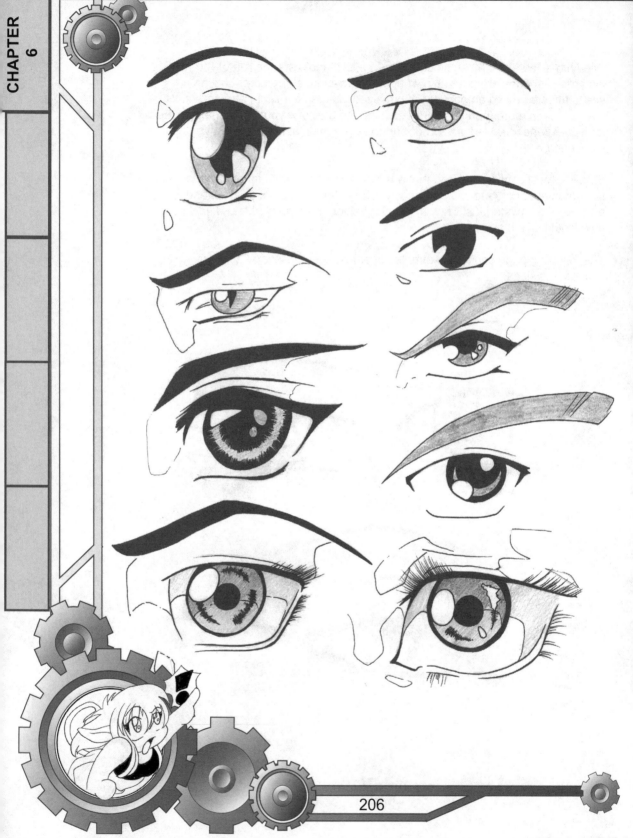

Not to overwhelm you, but there is still yet another feature to anime eyes. Sometimes the ways in which the eyes are rendered convey to the viewer the character's state of mind. Eyes made up of a solid color or a flat gradient imply that the character is in some sort of trance or is blind. Eyes with stars can signify a character that is literally "starstruck" with awe, and hearts can signify infatuation, obsession, or love of either another character or something inanimate. In Kiki's case, her heart-filled eyes are meant only for pies.

Spirals in the eyes can indicate the character is dizzy, or they can be used for comedic effect to show the extreme thickness of a nerd's glasses. Solid white circles with dark rims replace the eyes during moments of extreme shock and disbelief. Literal rivers of tears spring from the eyes of crying or overjoyed characters.

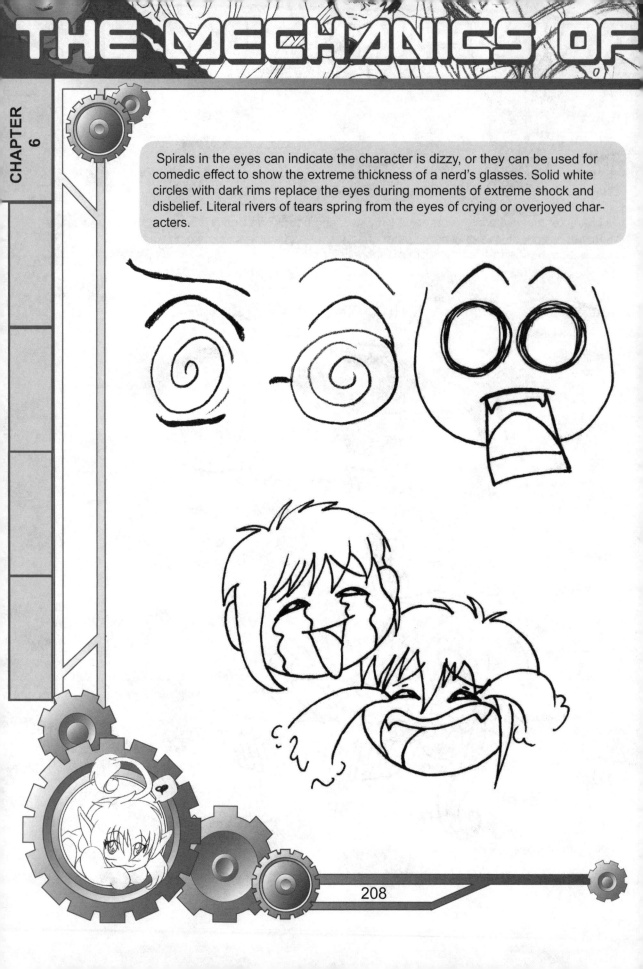

Half-moon shaped eyes can convey skepticism, while bubbly black eyes are a sign that the character is about to or already is crying. Large, round eyes with pinpoint pupils tell the viewer a character is shocked almost as much as the character with dark rims. Many more expressions exist in the realm of anime eyes, and it would be almost impossible to list them all. Add this to the fact that many artists have their own ways of interpreting these actions, and the list is endless.

Expressions
The following pages show the same character with different expressions applied. We did not change anything but her face, so note the different emotions she can display.

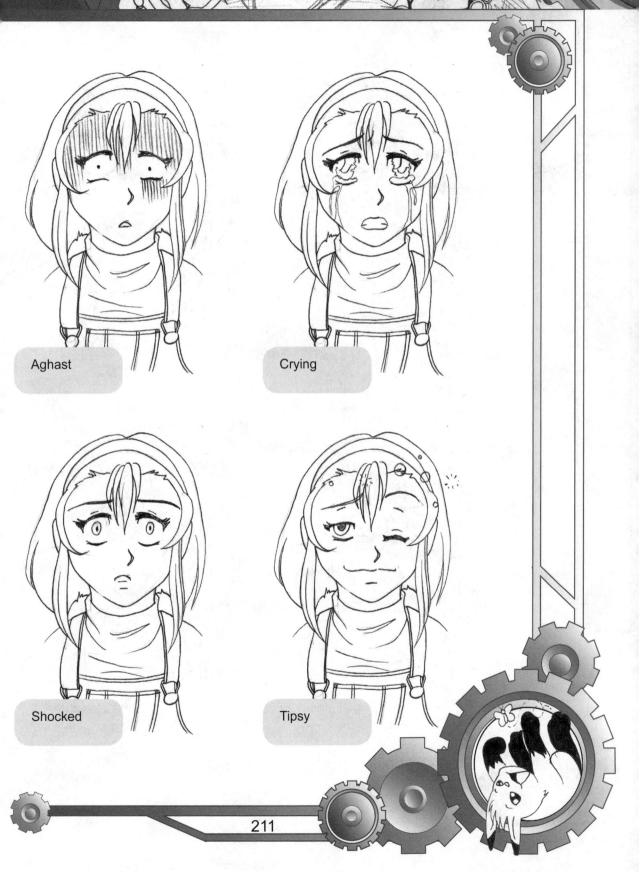

Aghast

Crying

Shocked

Tipsy

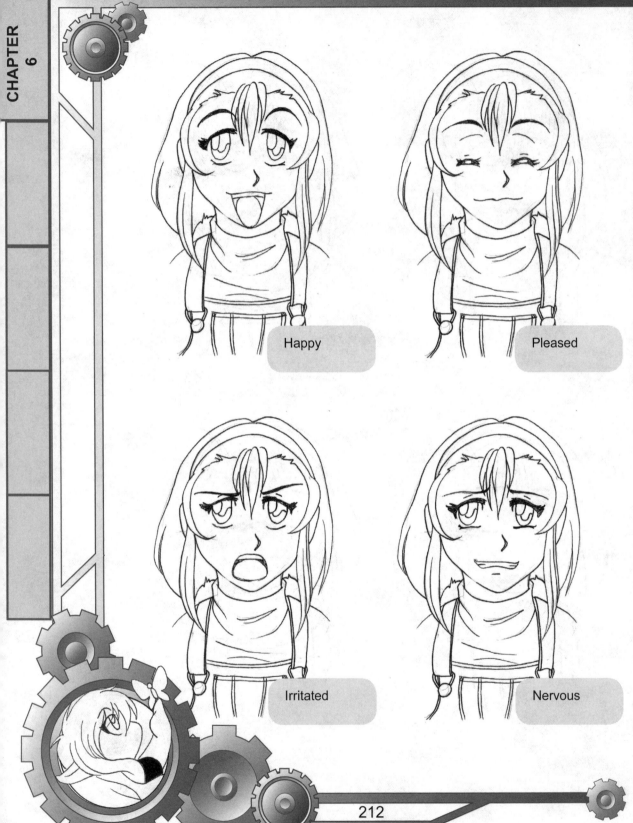

Happy

Pleased

Irritated

Nervous

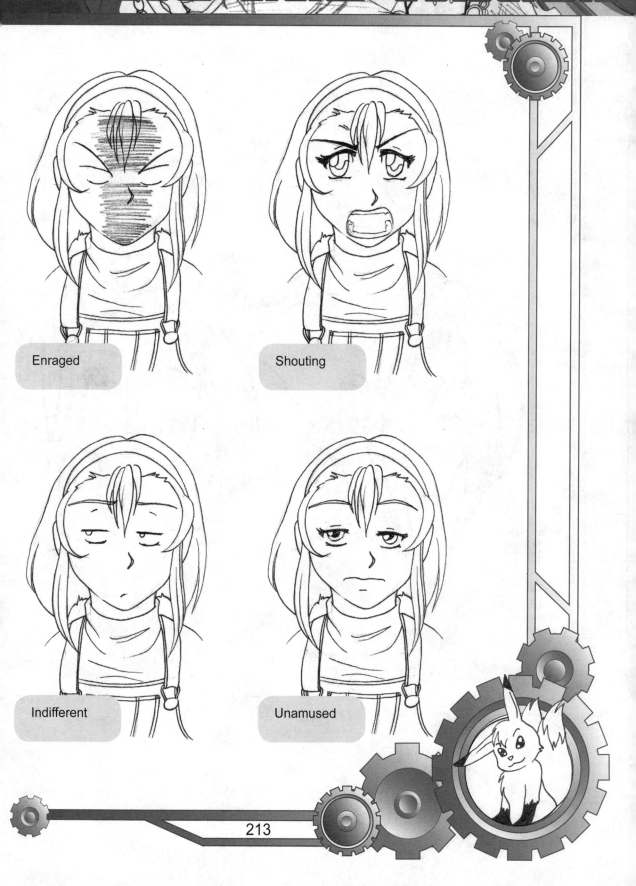

Enraged

Shouting

Indifferent

Unamused

Hair

Hair in anime and manga are two different animals. Anime hair is usually in solid chunks for ease in coloring and continuation from movement to movement. Manga scenes can cut from one pose to another without having to show that movement and are therefore allowed more freedom with fine lines, tone, and hatch marks.

Check out these three different hairstyles:

Point: All locks of hair originate from a single point.

Part: Hair originates from the part line.

Freestyle: The hair does not originate from any specific point, but remains "believably" close to the skull.

Point

Part

Freestyle

Hair in anime is a very mutable piece of your character that can express a lot about who and what he or she is. Color, style, and even the amount of hair your characters have can affect the viewer's perceptions of them.

Take the illustration of this little girl. Notice the big, puffy bangs and the playful little ear-tails that hang down the side of her face? Everything about that hair says "playful and innocent." Contrast this to our villainess, who has a very short, close-cropped look. Everything is controlled, cut in straight lines, and stiff. This haircut shouts "power," and she has a lot of it.

Even haircuts on males can convey personality. Our villain is wearing his hair in such a way that it at least partially covers his eyes. This puts a barrier between him and the audience. Not only is his expression standoffish, but his hair is too. The same principle can be applied to an anti-hero who would rather you think of him as a scoundrel than a saint. Now look at the stereotypical hero. His hair is trimmed and neat, or long and managed, but both styles look groomed and proper. Trimmed and neat says "boy-next-door" while long and kept says "nobility," but both can say "good guy."

Again, if your storyline allows, stir it up a bit! Give the anti-hero a crop top or give the villain long, lustrous hair. Just don't do it randomly. Do it for effect!

Hair Color

In anime, some characters are best known for their outrageous hair colors. For the artist, here is where creativity and some basic color theory can give your character yet another dimension. For a basic breakdown of colors, think of your blondes as anything from white to dusty brown or yellow-orange. Think of redheads as those with shades of hair from orange to red, and all the tints and hues that follow like pink or magenta. Brunettes are browns or cold colors. This includes everything ranging from purple to blue and green to black.

Here is where color theory comes in. However, remember that other cultures view colors differently than Americans do. So please bear with us on this one. Here are a few archetypal color and character designations:

• Red and other warm colors, like orange and magenta, usually portray a fiery personality. Sometimes these characters are mischievous or hot tempered, but they are loyal and passionate about their causes.

• Pinks, lavenders, and other pastel colors can represent innocence. Think of kids and cotton candy and the kinds of feelings those colors evoke.

• White, while representing purity in America, can also represent coldness and sterility. Characters with pure white hair or light blue hair can be considered cold and vicious, or pure and quiet, depending on the interpretation.

• Lighter colors, like blondes, can also convey purity and innocence.

• Dark colors of any shade tend to convey a learned or mature personality. Many times some of the older, wiser anime characters are given black hair with highlights of other colors to suit them.

Torso

Though there are significant differences between males and females in the way their torsos are drawn, they all begin with three circles. For a female, draw three circles roughly the same size with the top two touching and the bottom one slightly overlapping the middle one. For a male, make all three circles overlap slightly, but make the topmost one the largest and the middle one a little larger than the smallest—sort of like an upside-down snowman. These differences are because men have larger chests with small pelvises and females have smaller chests and larger pelvises. Go over the top and bottom balls with wedges. This helps you shape your character's gender into their body.

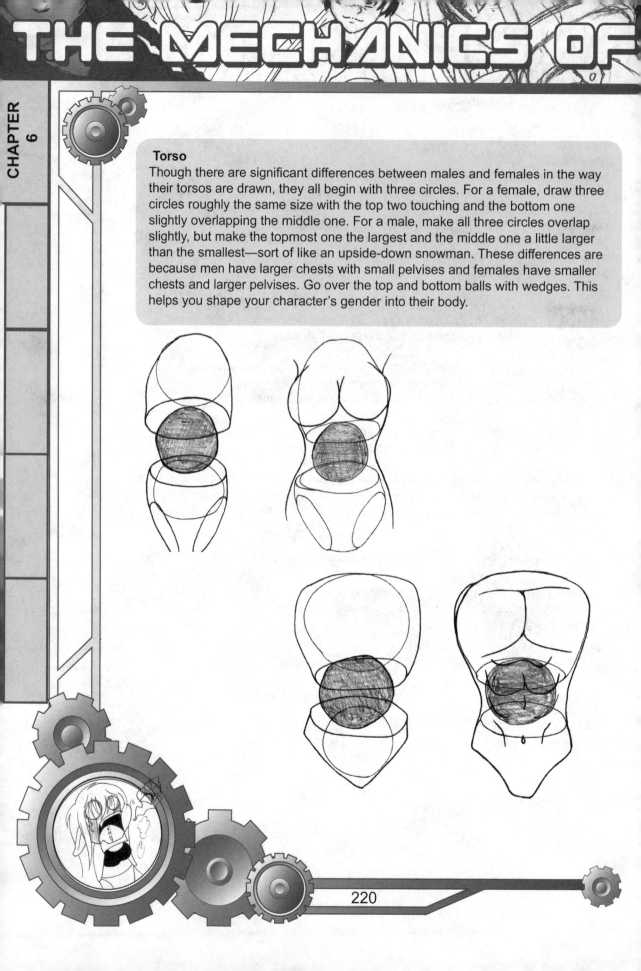

These figures show generic torsos in different positions. Note how the chest and pelvis wedges rotate around the torso ball.

Arms

The humerus, which is also called the funny bone, is the long bone in the arm that runs from the shoulder to the elbow. On a skeleton, it fits between the scapula (which is the shoulder bone) and the radius and ulna (the two bones in your forearm). As a general rule the humerus should be the same length as the forearm (the radius and the ulna). Some characters may have exaggerated lengths, i.e., large/long forearms to show strength or long/exaggerated humerus bones to make room for disproportionately large biceps.

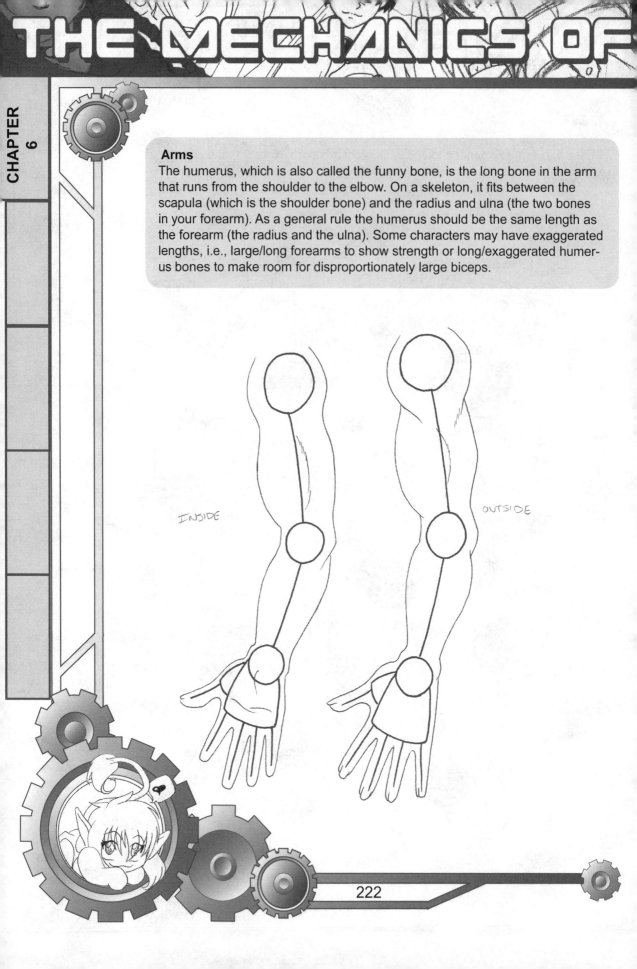

INSIDE

OUTSIDE

Check out the different positions of these arms.

Hands

Hands can be more complicated than you think. The average human hand has 27 bones. There are eight in the wrist, five in the palm, and 14 in the fingers and thumb. When drawing, you don't have to draw each and every one, but it's still good to know they're there. Place small circles where your joints are and large circles to represent the palm and wrist, connected or overlapped accordingly. Add a wedge around the palm and through the wrist circle to better represent the shape of the hand before outlining. There is your hand!

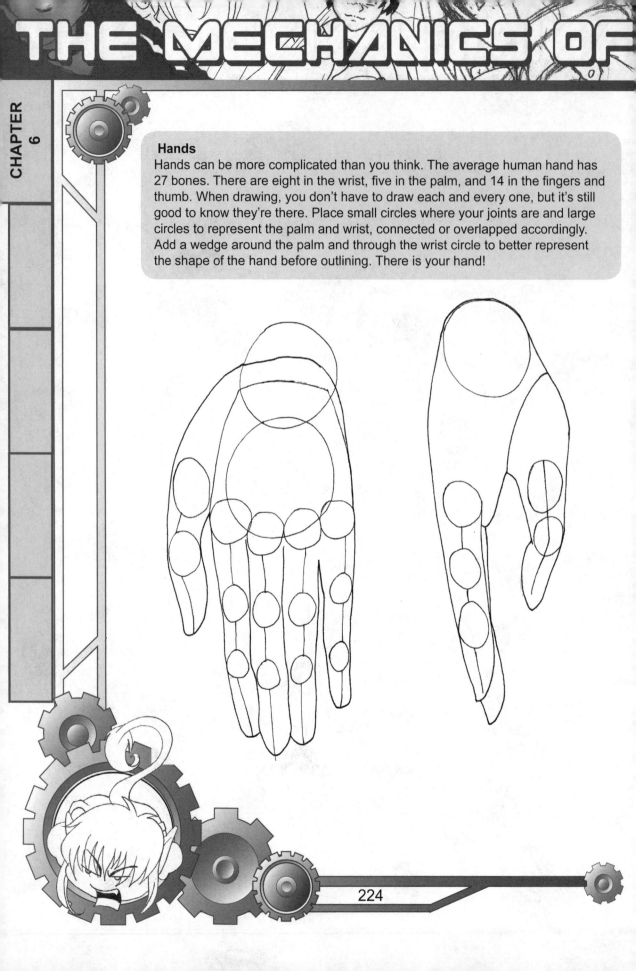

Here is an array of hands, all in different positions. Notice how some joints were omitted. If it is not important for the pose, you don't have to include it.

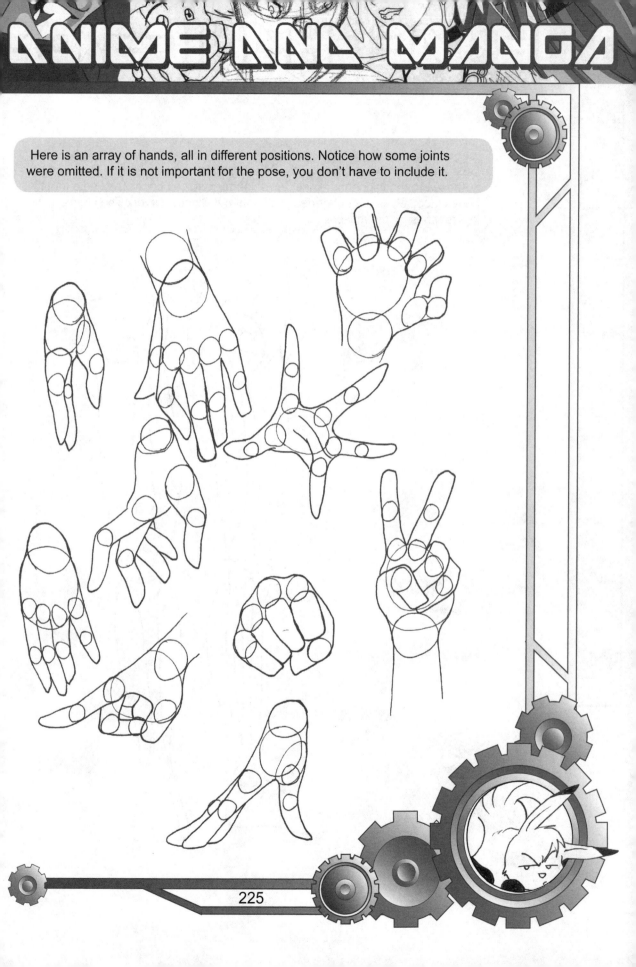

Legs

Legs are composed primarily of the femur, patella, tibia, and fibula. Respectively, those are the thighbone, kneecap, shinbone and calf bone. Take note that the bones themselves are not perfectly straight but slightly curved. The shape of the leg depends on the muscles.

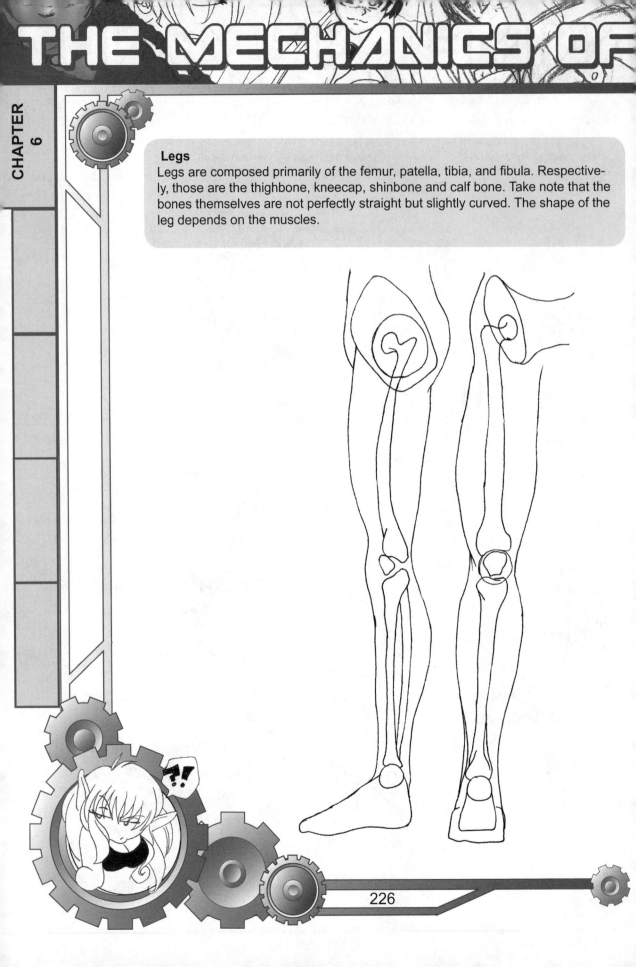

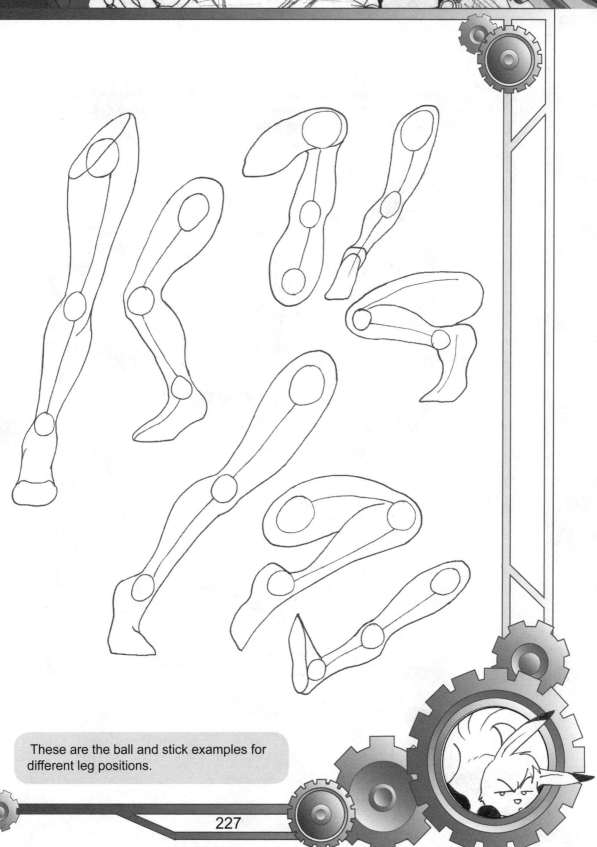

These are the ball and stick examples for different leg positions.

Feet

Feet are pretty simple. Just know where the joints are. You don't see barefooted characters too often. What is most important about the feet, however, are how the joints work with the placement of the foot.

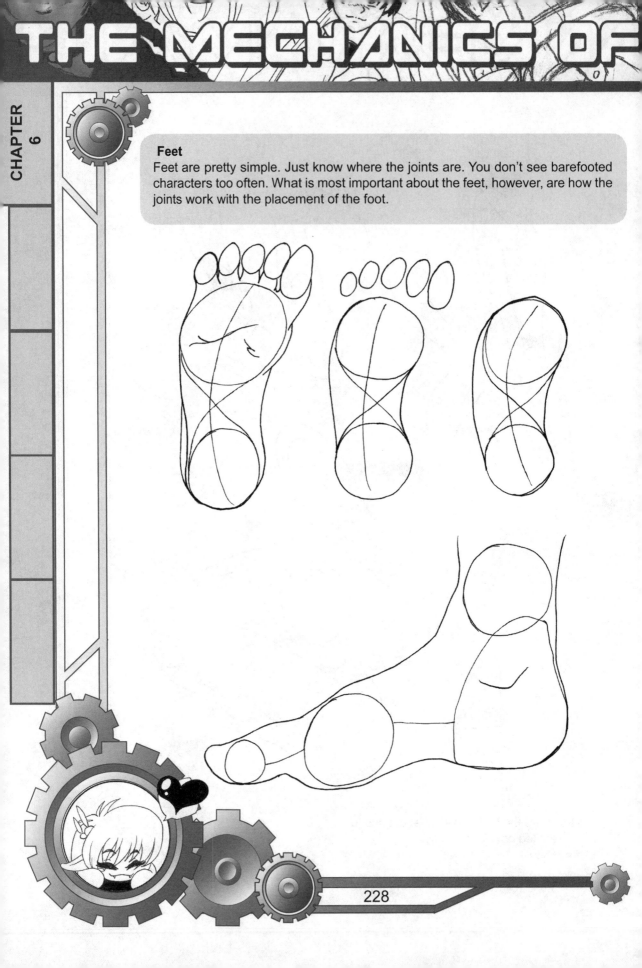

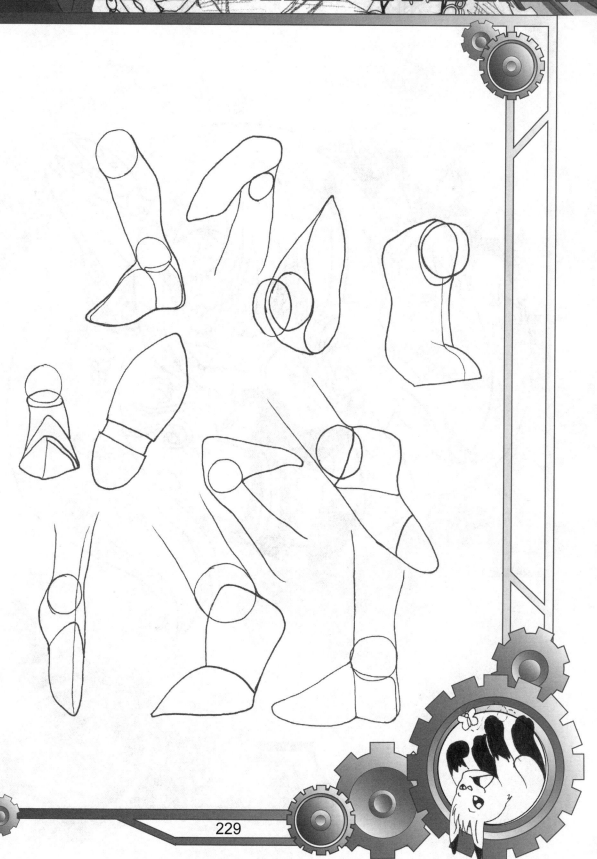

7

- Costuming
- Props

Aesthetics

Aesthetics are the attributes that make your characters visually pleasing. It can be the curve of their body, the sweep of their hair, or the shape of their face. It can even be in their movements or the expression on their face. Their clothing and accessories help, but are secondary to the character itself.

All the personality in the world will not make an automatically good-looking character. Although it is true that beauty is only skin-deep, unless that is the main focus of your story, we strongly suggest you take aesthetics into consideration. Unless there is a very specific justification as to why your character is not attractive, make him so. What draws in viewers is what is enjoyable to the eye. Most viewers will overlook or even ignore something that they either cannot identify with or is not "eye-catching" enough.

Look at other characters and try to identify what is appealing about them. Whether it is their delicate heart-shaped face or hulking muscles, you should recognize what makes characters look good. This will help you decide what sorts of traits you want your own character to have. Now that brings up the question, "What is visually pleasing about your character?"

Costuming

Clothes make the man…or woman, for that matter. How your characters dress can say a lot about them. Are they conservative or wild, traditional or radical? Take a look at some of the characters at Chapter 3, "Conceptualization," again. What does their clothing say about each character? Also, does the character dress in a way that is contrary to the way he or she acts, thinks, or feels?

If a character is a cute little girl who dresses in skins and armor but is more accustomed to flouncing about the market, the effect is comedic parody. It is a little girl pretending to be a warrior. Conversely, if the same little girl dresses in armor and skins but secretly harbors innate and tremendous talents in martial arts, the effect is still comedic, but it is that she is a little girl who kicks some serious butt.

Whichever way you choose to clothe your character, remember what the viewer's impression of him or her is and take it into consideration.

As for the physical act of clothing your character, take into account things like the transparency of materials, glossiness, and textures. A sheer overshirt will not have the same type of movement or effect as something like a wool cloak.

Shiny

Note the differences between the dull and shiny images.

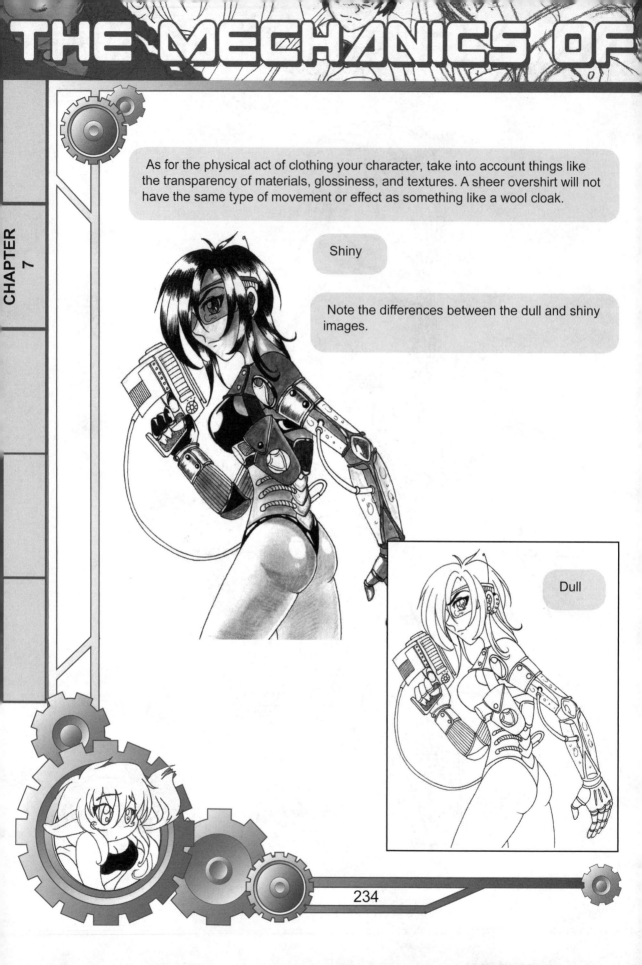

Dull

The next couple of drawings illustrate transparent versus translucent versus opaque clothing.

Transparent

Translucent

Opaque

Props

Props are anything found on a character that is not costuming or jewelry. This encompasses a lot and includes but is not limited to: weapons, tools, bags, and purses. Basically, it is everything but the character itself and what it's wearing. The best way to learn how to reproduce a prop is to get a live reference. The little things count, and realizing that even the props are made up of simple shapes is priceless knowledge.

For this particular guy, references were used not only for the dynamic pose of his arm, but even for the pencil in his hand.

The pencil is simply a series of cylinders, but things like the ridges in the grip, the clip, and the tip of the eraser head all add depth to the object.

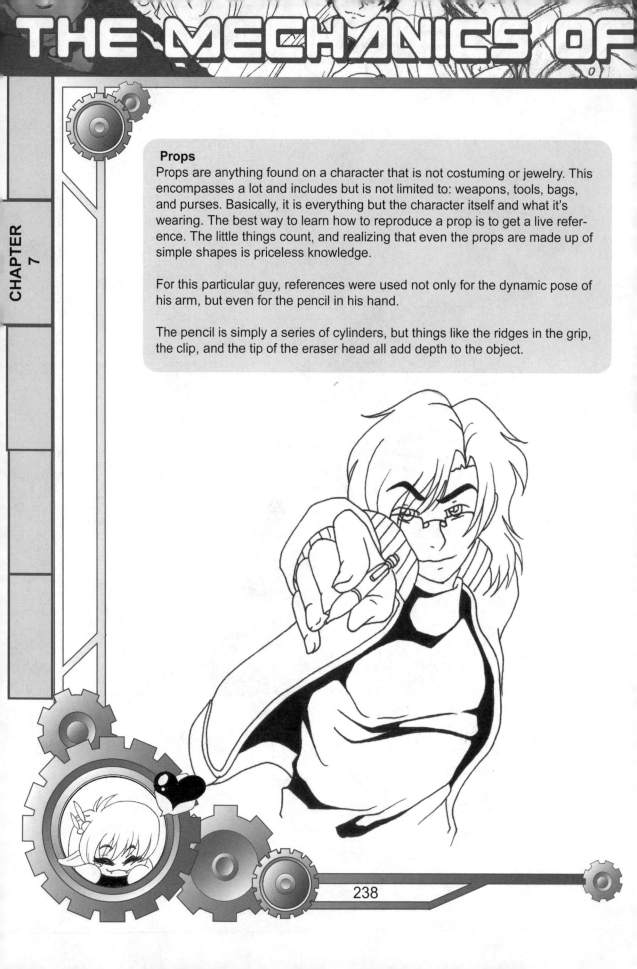

PENCIL AND INK WORK

8

- Laying Down an Image
  - Pencil Over Blue Line Before Ink
  - Inking Directly Over Blue Line
  - Pencil to Ink without Blue Line
  - Cleaning Up Line Work
  - Tiny Details

Laying Down an Image

Now that you know how your character looks, have studied its physical and psychological aspects, and have roughed it out, you need to finalize it. There are many ways to go about this depending on the final application of the character. If the character is actually destined for 2D animation, a solid pencil line is needed to constrain the colorist's bucket fills. If the character is intended for print or manga or is a conceptual piece, the options are much broader. The pencil can be cleaned (digitally or manually) or one of several different inking styles can be applied.

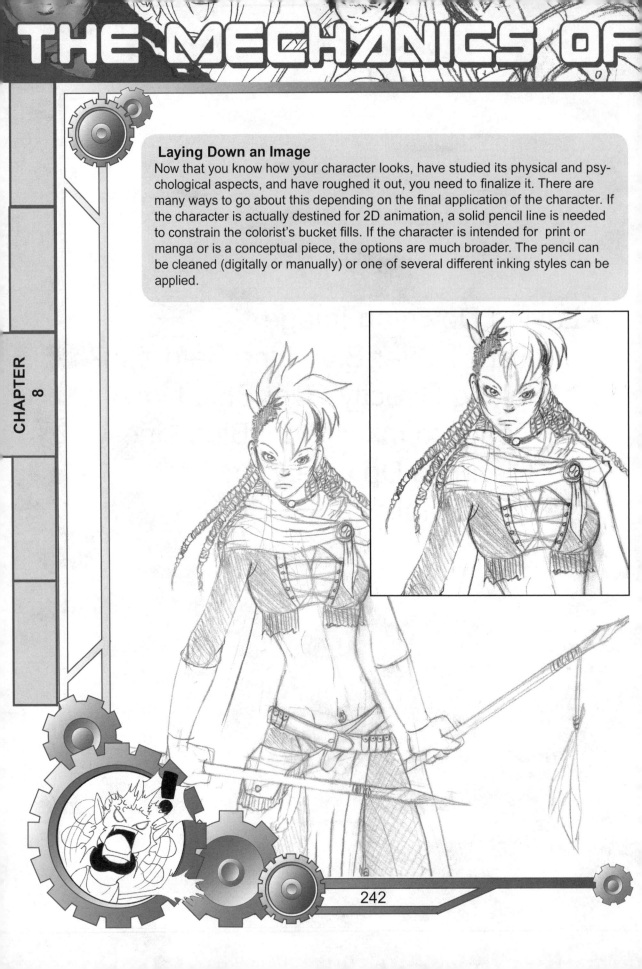

Pencil over Blue Line

The first technique is pencil over blue line. This is one of the few options for a character destined for animation. Traditional animation follows all of the steps shown in this book, but the final step (done by a cleanup artist) is always the same. A cleanup artist takes the rough (done either in non-repro blue, red, or green) and places it on a light table where he traces only the lines that are wanted with a dark, consistent pencil line. This has been done for animation for years, but the same principles can be applied to print media. Ink can be applied over the pencil if desired, but only if the character is destined for print.

Inking Directly over Blue Line
Another technique is ink over blue line. If the character is drawn from the line of action all the way to the rough in non-repro blue, one can ink over the non-repro blue, copy the image, and the blue under-drawing will disappear. Again, because this technique uses ink, it can be used only for print work. However, as further described in Chapter 9, "Inking," applicable inking techniques offer a great variety for all tastes.

Pencil to Ink without Blue Line

One of the most common print techniques, one used by manga artists and comic artists the world over, is inking over pencil. In this technique, the character is taken from the ball and stick figure to the rough figure in pencil. Ink is then applied directly over the graphite. It is a quick and common technique, but it can have a few drawbacks. Pencil can smear, especially if an artist is left-handed and is forced to use a right-handed sketchbook. Also, too many layers of pencil can obscure details, making the figure difficult to ink.

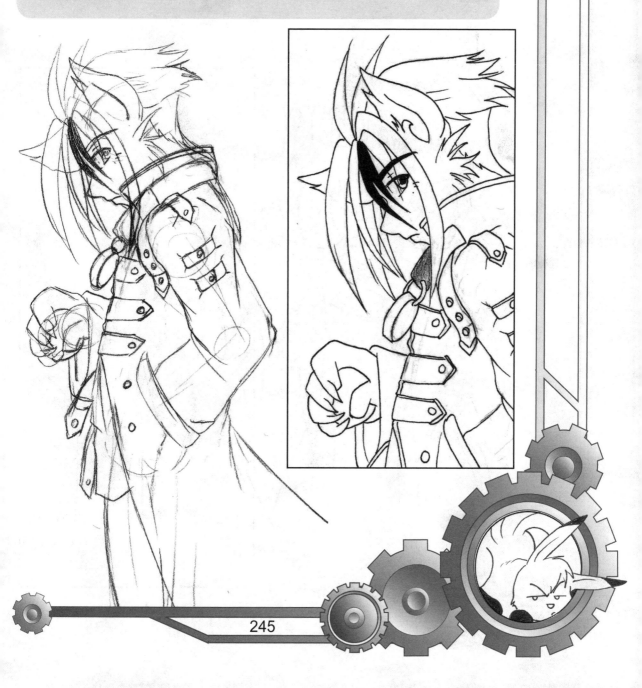

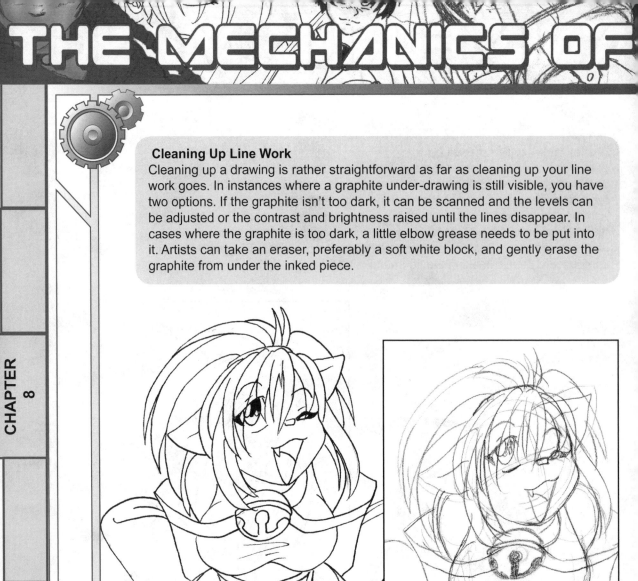

Cleaning Up Line Work
Cleaning up a drawing is rather straightforward as far as cleaning up your line work goes. In instances where a graphite under-drawing is still visible, you have two options. If the graphite isn't too dark, it can be scanned and the levels can be adjusted or the contrast and brightness raised until the lines disappear. In cases where the graphite is too dark, a little elbow grease needs to be put into it. Artists can take an eraser, preferably a soft white block, and gently erase the graphite from under the inked piece.

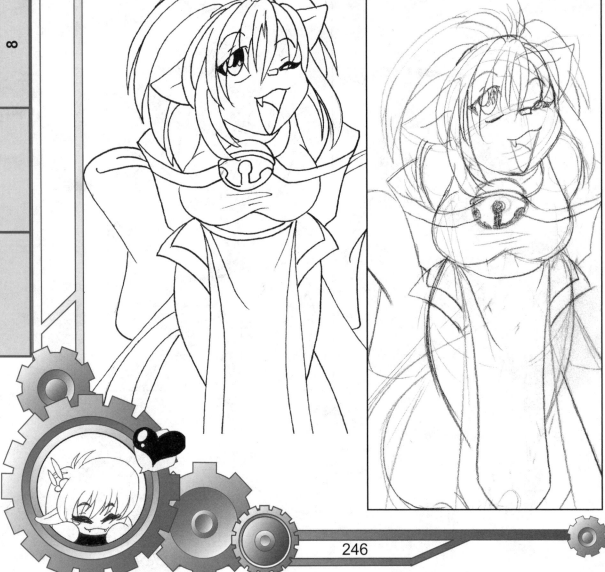

Tiny Details

At this stage, it is a good idea to check over your character one last time prior to the color stage. Sometimes little things like jewelry, hairpieces, or tiny baubles that were forgotten in the pencil stage can be added before they become a hassle to include in the color stage. Also, check for broken lines. If they were not intended to be there, it's better to take care of them now.

- Applying Ink by Hand or Computer
- Make a Light Copy
- Flat Ink
- Thick to Thin, Dark to Light
- Crosshatching
- Mostly Black
- Screentone Style

Applying Ink by Hand or Computer

There is not much difference in inking by hand or by computer. They follow the same principles and techniques; there are just different lists of pros and cons for each.

Computer inking has the magic of the undo command, a very handy thing indeed. Also, you do not actually use ink until you go to print. Unfortunately, inking with a mouse is unnatural, uncomfortable, and ultimately annoying. Inking with a pressure-sensitive tablet is much easier and less aggravating, but a tablet can cost as much as $300. Additionally, unless you know how to change the brush settings in your program of choice, thick to thin lines can be a challenge.

Inking by hand not only feels more natural, it is more natural. Plus, pens are cheaper than tablets, running between $2 and $4 apiece. However, you will run out of ink or the tips can fray with prolonged use.

Pen Ink vs. Digital Ink

Ultimately the choice is yours, but remember to focus on and practice with whichever inking medium you choose. With time and practice, both media will become easier to work with.

Make a Light Copy

A technique used by most graphic designers (as they are more accustomed to using vellum parchments and tracing papers) is to copy the image onto tracing paper with a darker line. This process is actually very similar to the light board techniques used by traditional 2D animators. A newer version of this print technique involves the computer. By scanning in a rough and lightening the lines, you can then print out the image and ink directly over it. This effectively creates an artist's very own blue lines. When rescanned, the scanner will pick up the darker inks but not the pencils below.

Flat Ink

Flat ink is a thin consistent line that outlines a drawing. This is probably the closest to the true anime style, as animation relies on such a consistent and dark pencil line for its color fills. Keep in mind that when inking, the line follows the pencil but is not necessarily constrained to it. Many things can change in the ink stage. Also, remember to keep the lines long and languid. You should practice making long flowing strokes.

Thick to Thin, Dark to Light

Thick to thin and dark to light usually go hand in hand as inking techniques. Pieces of a character or object that are closer to the viewer are darker or thicker than those farther away. For people with a lighter hand, light to dark may be a better option, but for those who have less control, thick to thin may be a better route. For either, it is best to start out with flat ink lines and either darken or thicken the lines closest to the viewer. Again, this can be done fairly effectively with practice drawings.

CHAPTER
9

Crosshatching

Crosshatching is probably the most complex inking technique. It is hard to master and if you make a mistake, it is very difficult to cover it up. Crosshatching is done in shaded areas, all in the same direction, and always away from the light source. The strokes involved in crosshatching are equally important. They are quick, short strokes that end with a point. Crosshatching can also have overlay lines. These are lines that flow at a 45° to 90° angle to the original hatching and provide the illusion of a darker shadow. Either way, crosshatching must be practiced, so we return to practice drawings…

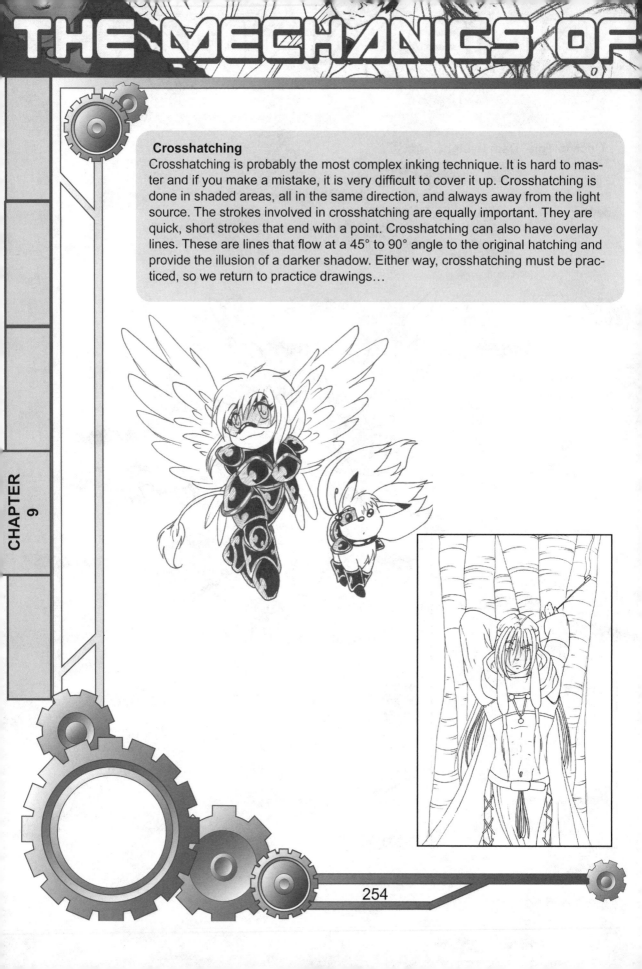

Mostly Black

This is a technique used by manga artists to give a "punch" to characters. Mostly black is a fill technique used over a flat inked/thick-to-thin/dark-to-light inked drawing. Mostly black is not all black. The rims of pieces (those surfaces affected by lighting) and lines that separate inside seams are bordered with white, almost as though the inside lines have been turned white on a black background.

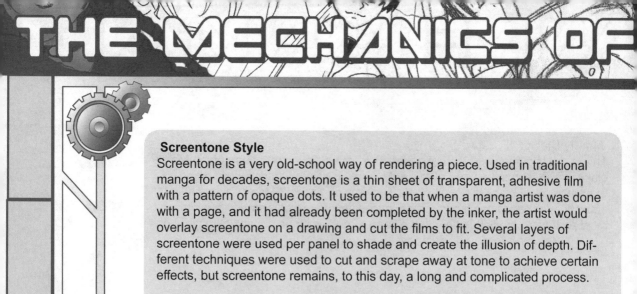

Screentone Style

Screentone is a very old-school way of rendering a piece. Used in traditional manga for decades, screentone is a thin sheet of transparent, adhesive film with a pattern of opaque dots. It used to be that when a manga artist was done with a page, and it had already been completed by the inker, the artist would overlay screentone on a drawing and cut the films to fit. Several layers of screentone were used per panel to shade and create the illusion of depth. Different techniques were used to cut and scrape away at tone to achieve certain effects, but screentone remains, to this day, a long and complicated process.

The advent of the computer changed all that. Screentone could now be scanned and affected digitally to create the same results as traditional tone, and because the original was never cut, artists could use the same sheet of tone over and over again. Overlaying screen became easier as well, because manga artists no longer had to worry about how thick their film was getting.

Since then, a few programs have come on the market that are specifically meant to achieve a screentone effect, but for the sake of this demonstration, we chose to used pre-scanned sets of screentone and Photoshop.

1. Scan in your pencil or inked piece.

2. Open or import your screentone.

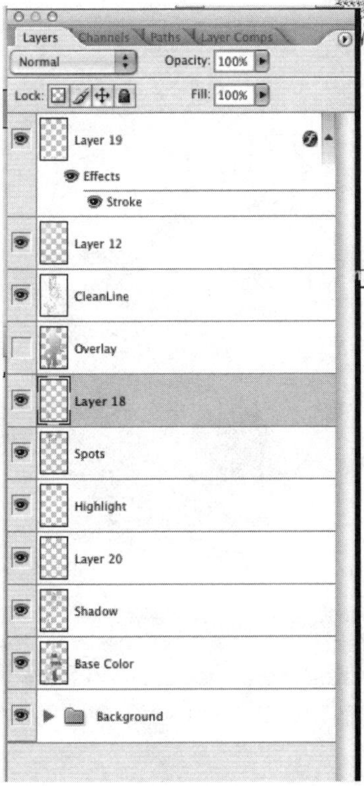

minmo bunny.psd @ 33.3% (Layer 1, Gray/8#)

Doc: 4.05M/7.66M

Layers | Channels | Paths | Layer Comps

Normal   Opacity: 100% ▶

Lock: ☒ ✎ ✛ 🔒   Fill: 100% ▶

Layer 19
Effects
Stroke
Layer 12
CleanLine
Overlay
Layer 18
Spots
Highlight
Layer 20
Shadow
Base Color
Background

3. Set the layer to Multiply. This should make all of the white on the screentone transparent, all the gray translucent, and all the black opaque.

4. Position the screentone over the area which you would like toned and erase the excess with the Eraser tool.

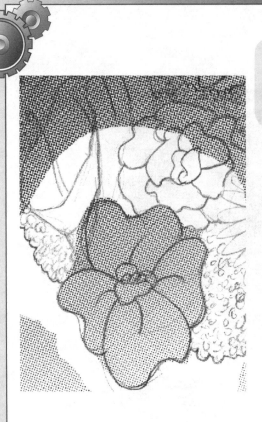

5. The process is repeated until the image is complete.

Some artists use a knife to scrape away tone to feather it or use a sand eraser to produce a gradation on the edge. This can be achieved digitally by using hard- and soft-edged erasers, respectively.

CHIBIS

10

- Chibis vs. Children
- Chibis vs. Super Deformed
- Chibis Compared to Actual Character
- Pick Out Main Elements
- Different Styles of Chibis

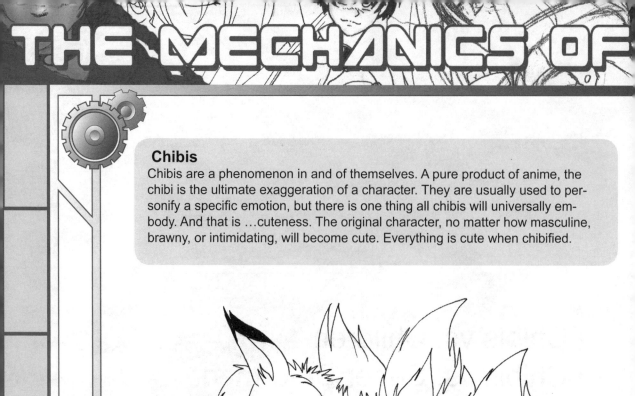

Chibis

Chibis are a phenomenon in and of themselves. A pure product of anime, the chibi is the ultimate exaggeration of a character. They are usually used to personify a specific emotion, but there is one thing all chibis will universally embody. And that is …cuteness. The original character, no matter how masculine, brawny, or intimidating, will become cute. Everything is cute when chibified.

Chibis vs. Children

Despite being child-like in appearance, chibis are not children. Chibis follow a set formula; that is, they are about three to three and a half heads high. Chibis are rather chubby like children, but are far more exaggerated and oftentimes a half to a whole head shorter.

Chibis vs. Super Deformed

While chibis are a form of super deformation, not all super deformed characters are chibis. Super deformed characters can have enlarged appendages or vary in head height from two to four heads. Chibis, as stated earlier, are only three to three and a half heads.

Chibis Compared to Actual Character

Chibi characters are an extreme exaggeration of their larger forms. They are shortened to three to three and a half heads and have stubby, simple limbs. Their heads take up the majority of their height and usually more than their width. The eyes are the dominant feature on the face, even when they were not on the original character, and the hands and feet are simplified sometimes to round nubs or rounded points.

It is the petite, rounded simplicity in its features that give a chibi its cute, childish appearance.

Pick Out Main Elements

To draw a chibi, one must first pick out the most important elements of a character. Chibis embody and exaggerate the features. If a character has a unique characteristic, such as a unique hairstyle or armor arrangement, keep them and exaggerate them. Let them shine! A chibi is the moment when even the coldest super-villain becomes a cute and cuddly character!

In Kiki's case, her wings and elven ears were exaggerated.

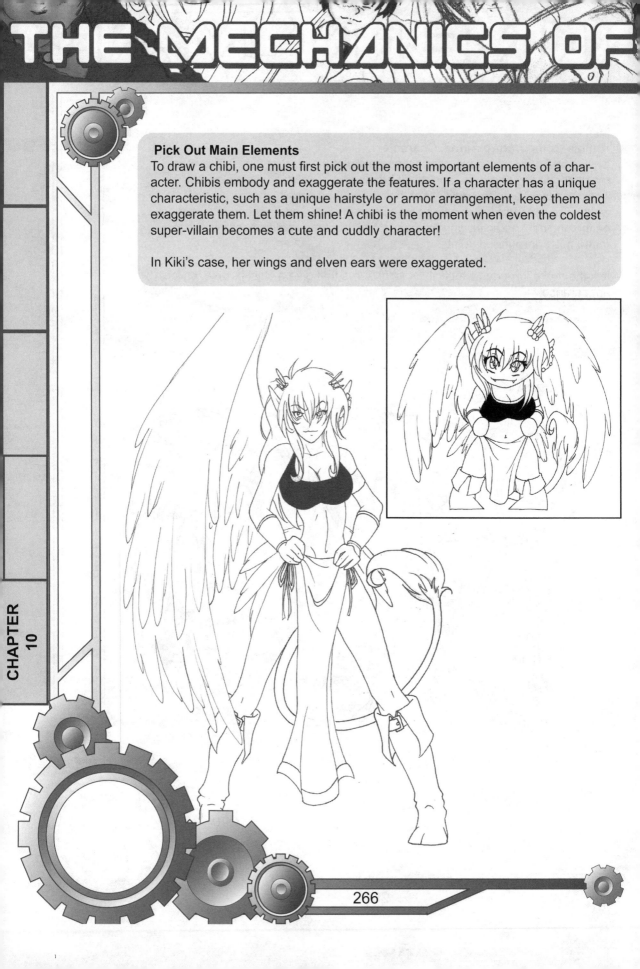

Different Styles of Chibis
These are examples of the different styles chibis can have.

- Cleaning Up Line Art
- Cel Shade
- Airbrush

Cleaning Up Line Art
Step one in any good piece of art—whether digital or traditional—is cleaning up your line art. For digital purposes, this can be done in a program such as Photoshop or Painter.

1. Scan your ink or finished pencil drawing.

See color
images
c1-c12

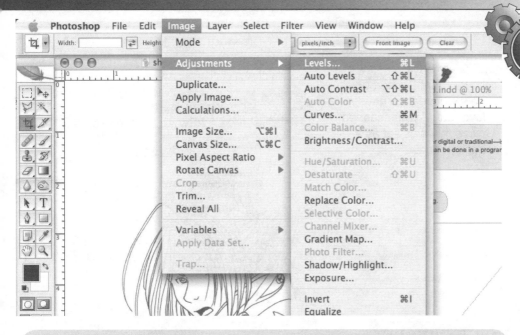

2. Go to Image -> Adjustments -> Levels, and move the small arrows as close to the edges of the histogram as possible. The objective here is to get lines as black as possible and a background as close to pure white as you can. If you notice your lines are becoming pixelated, you have pushed your levels too far.

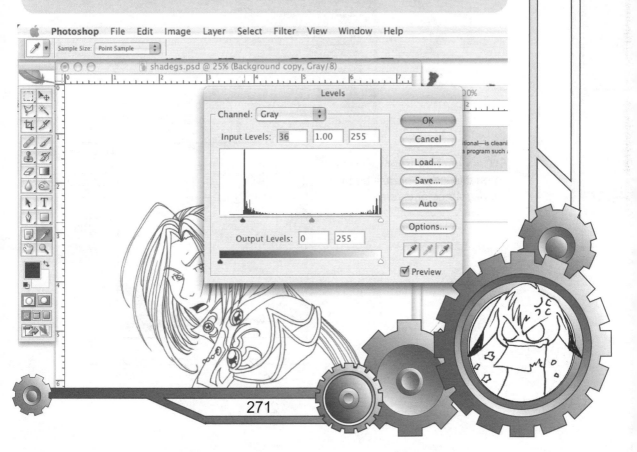

3. Go to Layer -> New-> Layer From Background. This will create a new layer out of your scanned piece that was set as a background.

Edit Image **Layer** Select Filter View Window Help

New ▶	Layer... ⇧⌘N
Duplicate Layer...	Layer From Background...
Delete ▶	Group...
	Group from Layers...
Layer Properties...	Layer via Copy ⌘J
Layer Style ▶	Layer via Cut ⇧⌘J
New Fill Layer ▶	
New Adjustment Layer ▶	
Change Layer Content ▶	
Layer Content Options...	
Layer Mask ▶	
Vector Mask ▶	
Create Clipping Mask ⌥⌘G	
Smart Objects ▶	
Type ▶	
Rasterize ▶	
New Layer Based Slice	
Group Layers ⌘G	

4. In this menu, set the layer to Multiply.

Normal
Dissolve

Darken
Multiply
Color Burn
Linear Burn

Lighten
Screen
Color Dodge
Linear Dodge

Overlay
Soft Light
Hard Light
Vivid Light
Linear Light
Pin Light
Hard Mix

Difference
Exclusion

5. Create a new layer by clicking on this icon. This will be the first of your color layers.

By setting the line art layer to Multiply, all of the black becomes opaque and all of the white transparent. Therefore, when you color the layer beneath it, it will seem as though you are covering the white but leaving the black. In reality, you just see through the white areas to the color beneath.

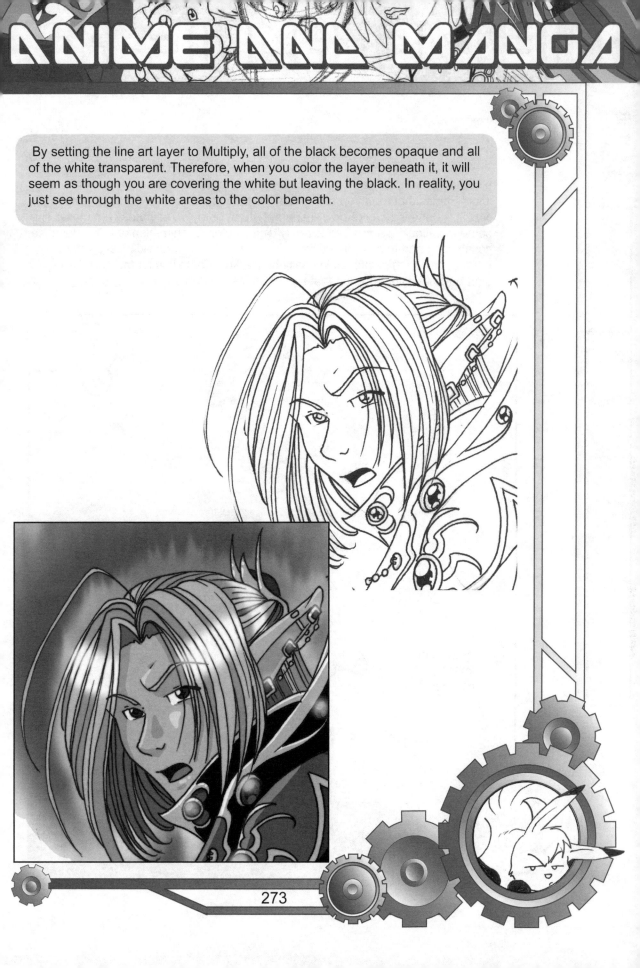

CHAPTER 11

Cel Shade

Probably the most unique thing to come out of animation is the cel shade technique. Originally, cel shading was the method by which painters filled in the celluloid frames that made up animation, the unique part of traditional cel coloring. Now it is done in reverse on transparent strata of Mylar, acetate, even glass. The same technique is now used to apply digital color for animation or print. Because cel shading had to be adapted for animation, colors were solid blocks whose edges or meeting points could easily be tracked. To do this for the digital age, we start out with a line drawing that has been cleaned up and is ready to go.

See color
images
c13-c26

1. Go into the Layer menu and select New -> Layer From Background to turn the line art into a layer instead of a background.

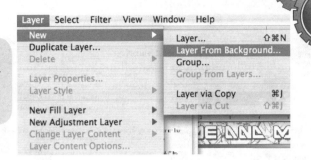

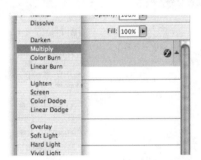

2. Set the layer to Multiply in the Layers palette. This means that all white areas of the image are now transparent, like the top layer of celluloid.

3. Create a new layer and…

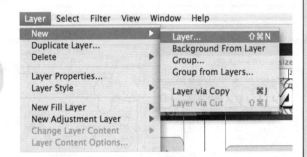

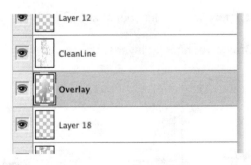

4. Drag it under the line layer.

5. Now you can color your base color with the paintbrush using a tablet or a mouse. Be sure to use a hard-edged brush. We are trying to imitate the bucket-fill look of digital cel shading.

6. Create another layer and…

7. Drag it between the line layer and your base color.

8. On this layer, paint your shadows.

9. Create yet another layer and…

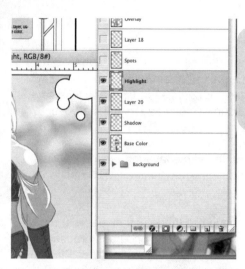

10. Drag it between the shadow layer and the line layer.

11. Paint your highlights on this layer, using a lighter version of the base color.

12. If you wish, you can create yet another layer and drag it on top of the highlight. This layer can be used as an ultra highlight on super shiny materials and is either an extremely light version of the base color or pure white.

Tips:
Since each piece of a composition (i.e., hair, boots, skin, etc.) will have at least three layers, it's a good idea to name them accordingly.
- On a PC, just right-click on a layer and change layer properties.
- On a Mac, click on the arrow on the Layers palette while the layer is selected.
- For print pieces, some artists take the Dodge tool at 20%-50% and lightly go over the base layer around the ultra highlights to add an extra "pop."
- Also for print, you can duplicate the line layer by dragging it to the new layer icon. Afterward, take the uppermost line layer and select it. Then, go to Filter->Blur and choose the Gaussian Blur. In this menu, set the blur between 2 and 5 to soften the line art. Hit OK and look at the difference it's made!

Airbrush

Airbrush is a recent painting medium compared to oil or watercolor. When airbrushing by hand, an artist masks off an area before airbrushing just one tiny section at a time. This creates beautiful blends but gets expensive and time consuming, and when you make a mistake you sometimes have to just start over and walk away from hours or days of work.

Enter the computer and the digital era. Using the same layering technique we used for cel shading, we eliminate the need to mask anything off and changes can be made in minutes.

The biggest difference between the airbrush and cel shade techniques is the way the color is used. Airbrush is a combination of subtle blends and gradations. Unlike cel shading, which has hard, edge-to-edge color, airbrush utilizes Photoshop's softer brushes to produce rich blends of color. Obviously the blends are not animatable, so airbrush remains a still technique.

1. First, we prepare our line art the same way we did in the cel shade section by changing the background layer to a normal layer and setting it to Multiply.

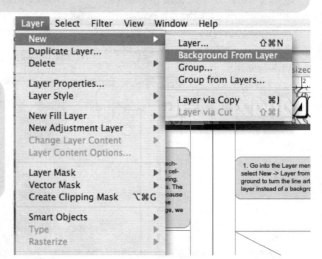

2. Next, we specifically designate a layer under the line art for each piece.

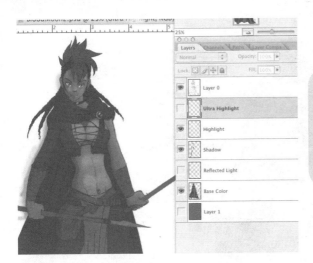

3. Then we use the same principle of light and shadow but with airbrush. The edges will be considerably softer, but this is understandable. Make the blend soft.

4. Here is something cel shading does not necessarily have: An added feature of airbrush, or any print for that matter, is reflected light. While it can be done in a cel shade, reflected light or bounced light is generally left for high-end animation (such as movies) or print material. Reflected light is caused by light bouncing off surfaces that are not necessarily highly reflective (i.e., a white wall or smooth plastic). The effect of reflected light is achieved by using a color slightly darker than the base tone but lighter than the shadow and a brush set at 50% or less opacity. Reflected light exists inside the shadow and usually rims whatever section of the character you are working on.

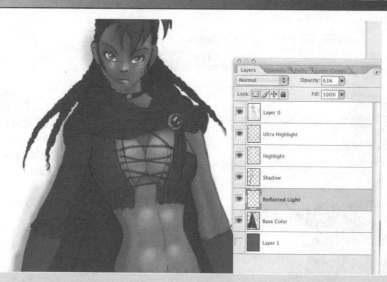

5. A close cousin to reflected light is rim lighting (sometimes referred to as contrast lighting). This is a colored light that is usually the complement of a color found in the character's skin tone or clothing. For example, this character's skin is a yellow or gold base; therefore, the rim light is purple to add more drama to the character. This is done within the reflective light, again with 50% or less opacity on the brush.

6. As with cel shading, this process is repeated over and over again until the image is completely colored. Be careful to pay attention to where your light source is coming from and do not deviate once it is set.

Airbrush is a more realistic painting style that gives very subtle shading transitions between colors to mimic the way skin actually looks to the eye. You can and should play with both to find the one that works best for you or use some combination of the two and find a totally different look that works best for your style.

See color images c27-c34

SPECIAL EFFECTS

- Weapon Fire and Energy Projections
- Glows, Reflections, and Magical Effects
- Inking Special Effects
- Screentone Special Effects

A large portion of anime and manga are the extreme special effects that make these media so unique and visually stunning. Special effects are anything the character does that is not directly seen as a native or natural occurrence, i.e., gunfire, energy blasts and manipulations, auras, magical effects, and so on. In our view, there are two basic types of special effects. The first are those directly connected to or within arm's reach of the character; we call these character interactive special effects. The other type of special effects are those that are at a distance; whether caused by the character or not, we call these environmental special effects. Explosions, area of effect magic (magic that affects a wide area as opposed to a single target), or weapon fire, and so on are all examples of environmental special effects. Extreme weather can fall into this category as well; whether it is a natural or unnatural occurrence depends on the circumstances and intent, but the effect can be extreme in either case and will require some type of special effects to pull it off correctly. We will go into greater detail about this category in the next volume of our "The Mechanics of Anime and Manga" series. For now we will concern ourselves with the character interactive type of special effects.

Weapon Fire and Energy Projections

Though vastly different in nature, weapon fire and energy projections can share some common ground in the way they are rendered. The illusion of a glow is caused by a high contrast between "pure white" and a secondary color. This is displayed quite well in things like laser beams, energy swords—almost anything based on an intense light effect. The core of an energy beam in most cases is white and has a harsh fade to the beam's color. A haze of color surrounding the projection renders a secondary glow.

Weapon fire uses the same principle of contrast between white and color. Weapon fire is rendered slightly differently from energy projection in that it sunbursts from the end of projectile weapons like guns, staffs, hands, and so on. This is achieved using the same gradation from white to the energy's dominant color, and a visible but slightly hazy version of the same color surrounding the effect.

See color images c35-c38

Glows, Reflections, and Magical Effects

Glow

Glows in digital programs are achieved with an airbrush type of effect when done for print. Try setting the airbrush at 10%-30% opacity and use it to rim that which is glowing. This is a versatile effect used not only in the previous section on weapon fire and energy projections but also in reflections and energy effects of magic items.

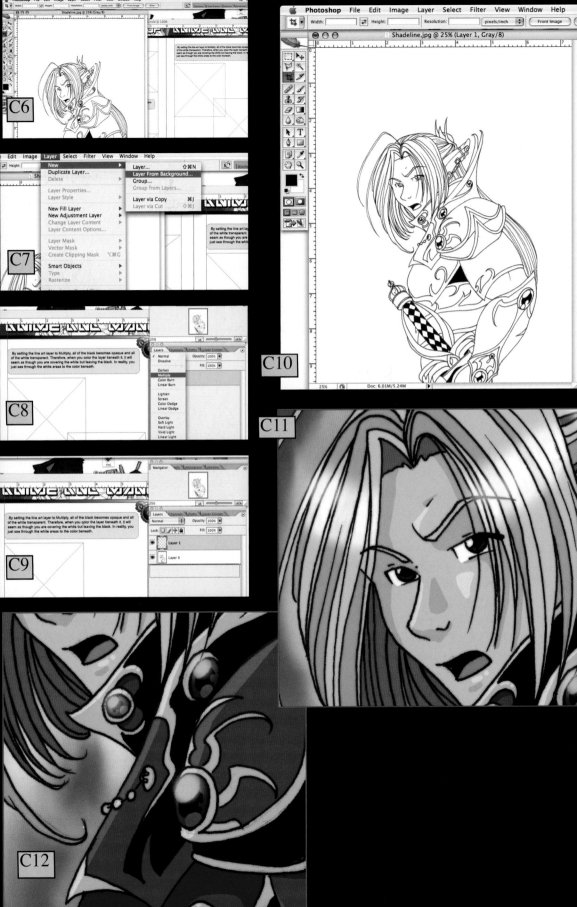

C28

C29

C30

C31

C27

C32

C34

C33

C35

C36

C37

C40

C41

C42

C43

C39

C44

C45

C46

C50

C51

C47

C52

C53

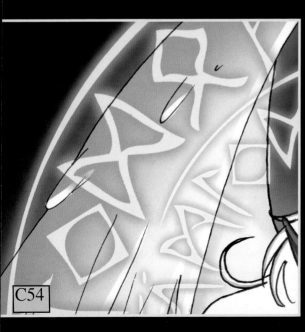

C54

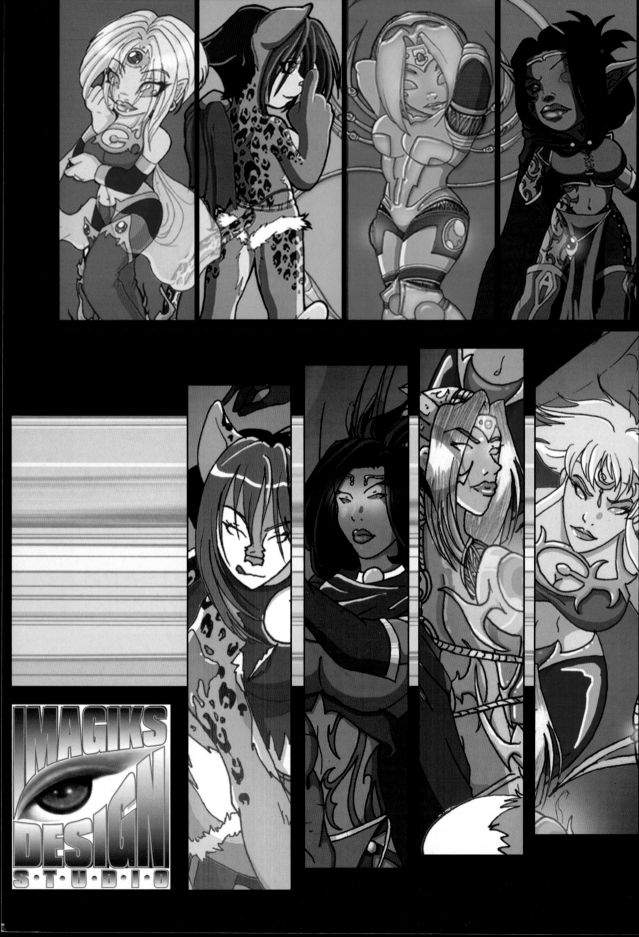

Reflections

Reflections are caused by shiny surfaces reflecting light in the shapes and colors of objects in its vicinity. While they can be clear representations, such as a mirror, oftentimes reflections are more obscure like those found in metals, polished stone such as marble, or watery/wet surfaces including a human's or similar creature's eye. In a digital program, reflections are made simpler in that one can temporarily flatten and then copy the subject and work the flattened version into the reflection.

See color
images
c39-46

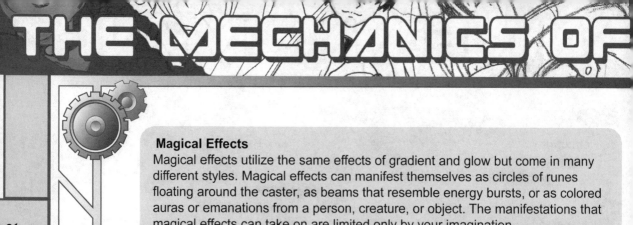

Magical Effects

Magical effects utilize the same effects of gradient and glow but come in many different styles. Magical effects can manifest themselves as circles of runes floating around the caster, as beams that resemble energy bursts, or as colored auras or emanations from a person, creature, or object. The manifestations that magical effects can take on are limited only by your imagination.

See color images c47-54

Traditionally in anime, a character that is able to manipulate energies predominately related to a life force or "chi" will exude a glowing aura. Since the character or core of the energy is not always white, the center of the aura is often transparent, creating a halo effect. In a digital program, this can be done by following these steps:

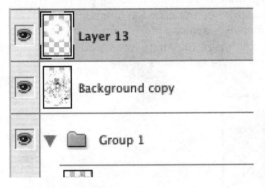

1. Create a new layer on top of your line art layer.

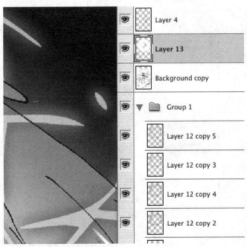

2. Instead of gradating your glow to white, utilize Photoshop's transparency abilities to fade to the background.

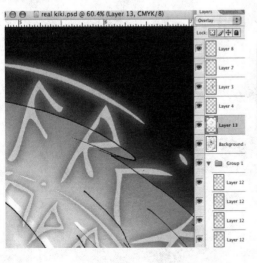

3. You may use the Smudge tool, the Blur tool, or several other techniques to fade the inside of the glow back into the background.

Inking Special Effects

Color, while prevalent in anime, is not the only way to render special effects. In manga, color is reserved for the beginning pages on a teaser, or not at all. As such, things like ink or screentone are used in its stead.

Inking special effects follows the same basic gradient pattern that regular glows do, but are achieved in black and white with solid black and white areas, as well as crosshatching. Check out this illustration. Notice that the energy whipping around has just as much inked detail as the character, and it uses the same principles of crosshatching explained in Chapter 9, "Inking." The crosshatching has been used to emphasize the amorphous state of the energy, as well as the gradient from the inside to the outer edge.

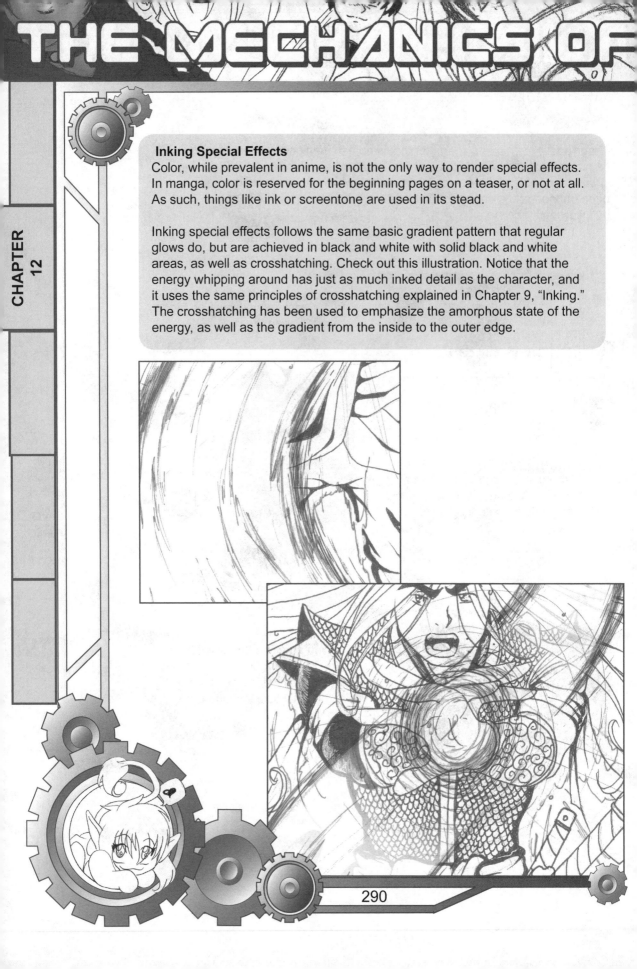

Screentone Special Effects

Screentone is somewhat simpler. Preset tones establish a gradient pattern that simply needs to be cut to fill the shape as illustrated previously in this book.

Keep in mind that even though the gradient is set with the screentones, the generated light by the source of the glow (i.e., the bright center of this glowing aura) and the ambient light still affect the character and should be taken into consideration when shading the character.

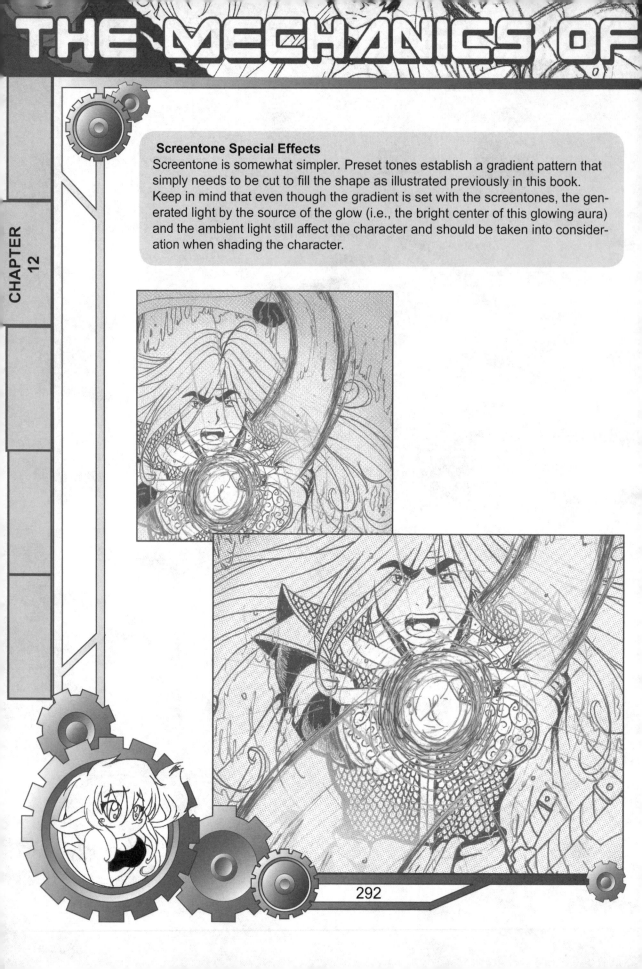

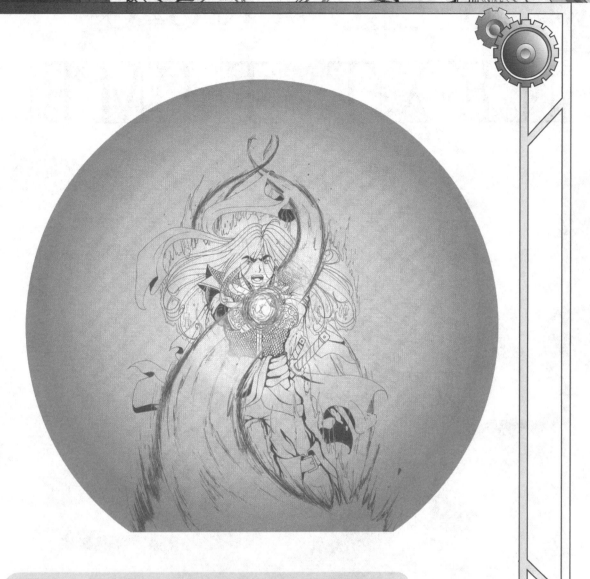

Special effects are the best way to bring drama and interest to your work. They are eye-catching and should always be very visually captivating. However, if badly done or overdone, your piece can quickly become garish, gaudy, or worse yet, cheesy. In most cases, special effects should be used to highlight an action and bring to a scene a sense of wonder. Or it can add drama to a given situation. Be very careful to not allow special effects to overpower a scene, unless that is your intent.

About the Studio

Studio Imagiks was conceived a few years before it was actually established, so in some form or fashion it has been around since the early '90s. Its current incarnation started in October 2001, when the shockwaves from 9/11 were still reverberating throughout the American economy. As one of many caught up in corporate restructuring, Damien Harrelson found himself with some extra time on his hands. At this point he made the decision to never again be in such a vulnerable position, so he started his own advertising and design studio, where he is creative director and senior designer.

From 2001 to 2005, he worked alone trying to establish his studio while working freelance for major Fortune 500 corporations including J.C. Penney, Texas Instruments, and Home Depot. Then the opportunity arose to bring in more help as interns. Having been a product of the educational system himself, Damien knew the pitfalls and traps that awaited those who graduated and stepped out, wide-eyed, into the world of advertising. Damien began taking interns to mentor them, with the goal of guiding them through and around the challenges they would soon encounter. So began Studio Imagiks as it now exists.

About the Authors

J. Damien Harrelson, Creative Director and Sr. Designer

Education: Bachelor of science with a minor in fine arts (painting), associate degree in design with an emphasis on airbrush illustration, and associate degree in digital design with an emphasis on image manipulation and photo-retouching.

Background: Damien Harrelson was born and raised in Texas. He started Studio Imagiks to avoid the whims and pitfalls of working for corporate businesses and to gain more control over his own career. Damien has been associated with Phoenix Entertainment and A-kon since 1991, becoming its art director in 1994 and executive director of exhibits and installations in 2002. Through his connection with Phoenix Entertainment, he has had dealings with some of the biggest names of Japanese pop music, anime, and manga for 17 years.

Christina Le, Lead Editor

Education: Bachelor of arts in arts and technology from the University of Texas at Dallas; planning to work on a master's in business administration.

Background: Christina Le has lived in Texas since 1998. She graduated from DeSoto High School in 2002 in the top 20 of her class. In college she started a degree in fine arts but switched to arts and technology. She was introduced to Studio Imagiks through one of its customers in June 2005. Christina first became lead editor for the purpose of "RAITH 2525" (title pending) but also worked on "The Mechanics of Anime and Manga" series. She currently resides in the suburbs of Dallas with her demonic kitty.

Jacquelynn M. Mumm, Lead Artist

Education: Applied arts degree in computer animation; working on applied sciences degree in digital media production.

Background: Jacquelynn Mumm came to Texas in June 2002 to get as far away from snow as humanly possible and to get her degree in computer animation. In August 2002 she began attending the Art Institute of Dallas. In June 2004, she was introduced to Damien Harrelson through a mutual friend. Committed to finishing her degree, she did not begin working with Studio Imagiks until January 2005. In late August, she was approached to continue with Studio Imagiks as the lead artist. Currently she is working with Studio Imagiks on "The Mechanics of Anime and Manga" series and "RAITH 2525" (title pending). Her other work for the studio includes package design for a line of aromatherapy products and promotional work for local trade shows and special events. This is on top of attending college full time for her second degree with an emphasis in digital art and video, which adds new skills to the studio arsenal. She currently resides in Richardson, Texas, with "four" cats.

Glossary

Android: A synthetically made humanoid.

Anime: An animation in a specific style. Originally, anime referred to Japanese animations, but now is a reference to the style.

Area of effect: A term for a magic spell or an attack such as a grenade blast that affects an area rather than a single target.

Ball and stick figure: A figure drawn to block out a character that takes the place of a skeleton.

Blue line: The blue under-drawing created with a non-repro blue pencil that does not photocopy.

Cel: A celluloid. Clear material upon which a traditional animator draws lines and applies paints to create a single frame of animation.

Chibi: A child-like version of a character. A chibi is from three to three and a half heads high and has simplified hands and feet.

Cyborg: Any manner of part human, part machine that retains a human intelligence.

Line of action: The primary line that defines the action or main movement of a character.

Manga: Japanese comics, most commonly characterized by the use of screentone and unique panelling techniques.

Oni: A mythological Japanese demon with a hideous exterior.

Pixel: A picture element. A square of color that, when set beside several others of its kind, creates a picture, kind of like a mosaic.

Pixelation: An effect caused when an image has been over-enlarged and the individual pixels are discernible.

Raster graphics image: An image composed of a series of colored pixels.

Ronin: Samurai without lords and are sometimes swords for hire.

Samurai: Any ranking warrior acting under the Shogunate dynasty and following the way of Bushido, the Japanese warrior's code.

Screentone: An inking technique that uses a thin sheet of transparent, adhesive film with a pattern of opaque dots.

Shojo: Manga and anime that is oriented toward girls. Often, there is lots of angst in the storylines.

Shonen: Manga and anime that is oriented toward boys. There are usually a lot of action scenes.

Super deformed: Any character in anime that personifies a deformed or exaggerated version of a character without being a chibi.

Vector graphics image: An image made up of lines that are actually algorithmic calculations of curves between two points.

Youkai: A mythological Japanese demon, sometimes with a beautiful exterior.

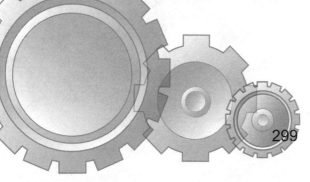

index

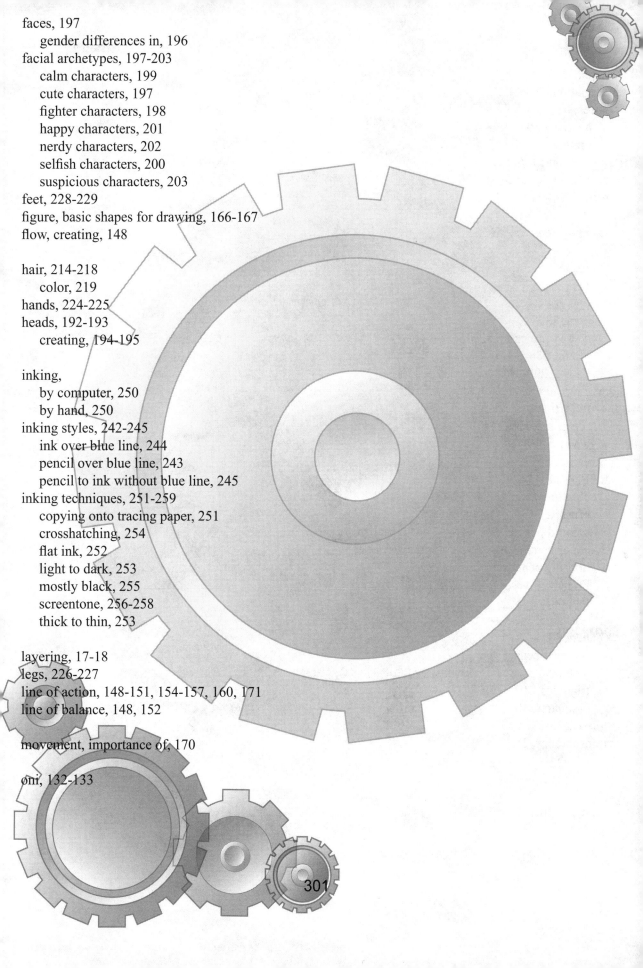

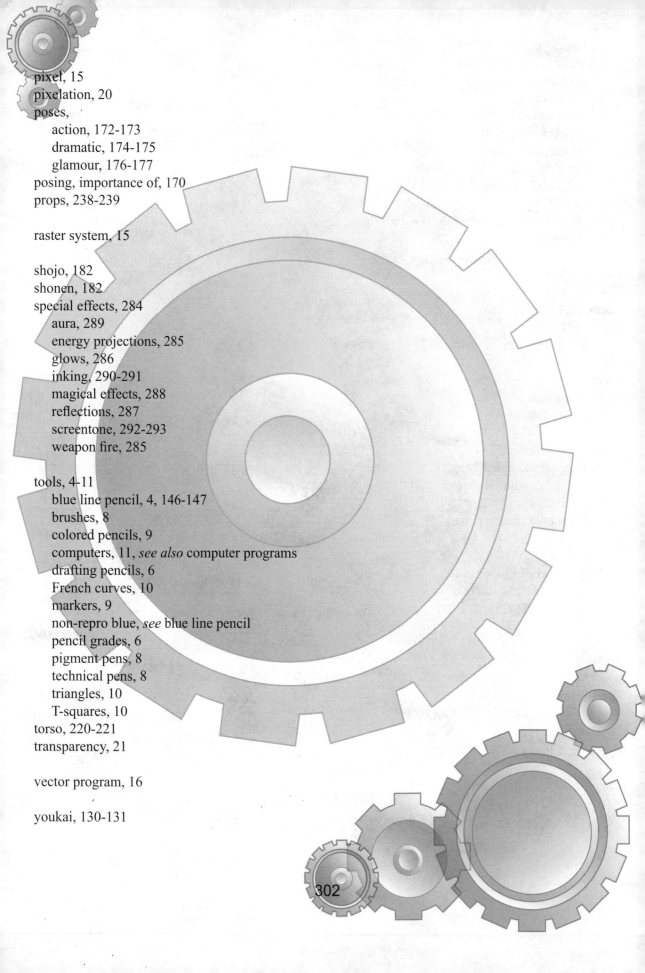